European structures
of qualification levels

A synthesis based on reports on recent developments
in Germany, Spain, France, the Netherlands
and the United Kingdom (England and Wales)

VOLUME 1

Anneke Westerhuis

Cedefop Reference series
Luxembourg: Office for Official Publications of the European Communities, 2001

A great deal of additional information on the European Union is available on the Internet. It can be accessed through the Europa server (http://europa.eu.int).

Cataloguing data can be found at the end of this publication.

Luxembourg:
Office for Official Publications of the European Communities, 2001

ISBN 92-896-0057-8

Designed by Colibri Ltd. – Greece
Printed in Belgium

The **European Centre for the Development of Vocational
Training** (Cedefop) established in 1975, provides information
and analyses of vocational education and training systems,
policies and research.

Europe 123
GR-570 01 Thessaloniki (Pylea)

Postal address: PO Box 22427
GR-551 02 Thessaloniki

Tel. (30) 310 490 111, Fax (30) 310 490 020
E-mail: info@cedefop.eu.int
Homepage: www.cedefop.eu.int
Interactive website: www.trainingvillage.gr

Anneke Westerhuis, *CINOP/s'Hertogenbosch*

in cooperation with:
Richard Koch and Jochen Reuling, *BIBB/Bonn*
Günter Heitmann, *Technical University of Berlin*
Joan-Anton Bruna, *Fundación CIREM/Barcelona*
Annie Bouder, Jean Louis Kirsch
and Thomas Coupié, *CEREQ/Marseille*
Joop Nafzger, *CINOP/s'Hertogenbosch*
Tim Oates, *QCA/London*

Edited by: **Cedefop**
Burkart Sellin, *Project Coordinator*

Produced under the responsibility of:
Johan van Rens, *Director*
Stavros Stavrou, *Deputy Director*

Preface

In all European Member States and highly industrialised countries, the structure of the labour force and the organisation of work are continuously changing. Technological, economic, social and educational developments, and the need for flexibility and more active and creative multi-skilled workers, as well as the reduction in the number of hierarchical levels in companies, strongly influence labour force structures. Education and training systems are challenged by these developments. They are expected to contribute actively to the creation of employment and jobs, and the restructuring of work organisation, and to reconsider the structure of qualification levels, etc. How precisely do these systems respond to structural changes in the labour force and work organisation? How do they take into account or contribute to these structural economic changes? More particularly, how do national qualification systems respond to these changes in terms of the number and definition of levels, types and character of qualifications?

In 1997, Unesco made an effort to revise the international standard classification of education (ISCED). ISCED had been designed as an instrument suitable for assembling, compiling and presenting education statistics, both within individual countries and internationally. The revision, undertaken by Unesco in close cooperation with the OECD and Eurostat, led to a revision of ISCED. The revised classification tried to achieve a balance between educational provisions and VET provisions [1]. For this reason, Cedefop and Eurostat developed a field of vocational training structure, which is basically an economic sector based classification of training programmes [2].

Cedefop emphasised the need for a reassessment of the 1985 European Communities five-level structure of training and qualification levels [3].

Does the European Community's five-level structure, which was retained by the Council in 1985 in terms of number and definition of levels, deliver sufficient criteria for classification?

Does the system sufficiently reflect present and future developments in education/training, in employment and changing work organisation and does it permit a cross-country or even a European-wide comparison and observa-

---

[1] See Annex 5.
[2] *Fields of training (manual),* Cedefop and Eurostat, Thessaloniki and Luxembourg, 1999.
[3] See Annex 2.

tion of current and future trends?

In the light of socioeconomic changes and new challenges for education policy and lifelong learning, it may be that stakeholders, policy-makers, social partners and educationalists in the Member States increasingly question the European five-level structure. To what extent, if at all, does this 1985 five-level structure still respond to these needs and should it be adapted to the changes which have occurred during the past 15 years?

To prepare and feed this policy debate, and in response to Cedefop's own work programme, this study was launched during the 1998 plenary meeting of Ciretoq, Cedefop's network for research cooperation on trends in occupations and qualifications.

It was agreed that an in-depth study of five national vocational education and training structures should be undertaken and cover three fields:

(a) an analysis of the characteristics of national qualification frameworks (number and definition of levels, definition of qualifications, criteria for classification, procedures for updating qualifications);

(b) an analysis of the similarities and differences between the national frameworks and the 1985 European five-level structure;

(c) an assessment of whether the European structure of qualification levels is being applied in the respective EU Member States and, if so, how and to what extent.

The study identifies trends and developments in some Member States in relation to national frameworks and their role in education/training and the labour market. It will feed the debate on whether, and to what extent, an update of the European five-level structure is relevant. It will support the decision-making process on the future of a European reference framework for training and qualification levels.

The study was conducted on behalf of Cedefop by *CINOP* (the Dutch Centre for the Innovation of Education and Training), by Joop Nafzger and Anneke Westerhuis, the latter ensured the technical-scientific coordination and the editing of this synthesis report in cooperation with *BIBB* (the German Federal Institute for Vocational Training), Richard Koch and Jochen Reuling; the Technical University of Berlin (Institute for VET and Further Education), Günter Heitmann; *Fundación CIREM* (the Spanish Foundation Centre for European Initiatives and Research in the Mediterranean*)*, Joan-Anton Bruna; *CEREQ* (the French Centre for Study and Research on Qualifications), Annie Bouder, Jean-Louis Kirsch and Thomas Coupié; and QCA (the Qualifications and Curriculum Authority for England and Wales), Tim Oates.

The study covers five countries/European regions: Germany, Spain, France, the Netherlands and England and Wales. The contributions on country-specific developments and outcomes are published in Volume 2 by Cedefop. These present an introduction to recent developments, discuss perceived problems relating to national standards, qualifications and classifications and form the basis for this report. Volume 3 focuses on recent developments in higher education concerning levels and qualification structures; these are marked by increasing differentiation yet also by a certain convergence in terms of a European and international comparability. This expertise, courtesy of Günter Heitmann from the Technical University of Berlin, complements both Volumes 1 and 2.

These reports should be viewed as expert contributions elaborated by *CINOP* and the authors under their own responsibility. The views expressed are not necessarily those of Cedefop, nor of the other participating institutes.

Stavros Stavrou
Deputy Director

Burkart Sellin
Project Coordinator

Contents

1. Introduction

1.1. Definition of concepts

One of the first questions to be answered when analysing and comparing classification systems is which framework(s) of each country should be included in the study. The definition and scope of classification frameworks vary greatly between EU Member States. What exactly is classified in a framework? How closely is the qualification framework linked to educational standards and the respective education and training system?

In England and Wales, the government, following the Dearing review of qualifications for 16-19-year-olds, introduced a national framework covering general secondary education, vocational education and training, post-initial training, work-based learning and prior learning (1998). Spain is working towards the introduction of a similarly comprehensive classification framework, while in France the introduction of an all-encompassing framework is being proposed to parliament. Germany, in contrast, does not have a comprehensive classification framework, nor is it working on one. Germany identifies a number of types of vocational education:

(a) education for the so-called recognised VET occupations (*staatlich anerkannte Ausbildungsberufe*);
(b) full-time and school-based programmes for the so-called educational occupations (*Schul-* or *Fachschulberufe*);
(c) national and federal state regulated continuing training occupations (*Weiterbildungsberufe*);
(d) tertiary education programmes (*Fach-* and *Hochschulberufe*).

Together, these education categories might be regarded as an implicit framework of qualification levels.

The position of the Netherlands is somewhere between England and Germany. It identifies two qualification frameworks; a formalised structure covering secondary vocational education programmes and an implicit structure for higher professional education, being a part of 'higher education' (*hoger onderwijs*). As in England, the aim is to use secondary vocational qualification standards for the assessment of prior learning as well as for continuous vocational training provisions. Both systems have their own procedures for developing standards and qualifications.

In France, the current grades of the Ministry of Education are the most traditional route to a qualification. They are organised (classified) within an architecture of levels and fields, which have a strong influence on other classification systems, both inside and outside the education system. Reform is on its way in Spain. A bill has been presented to the national assembly, proposing to set up a cohesive, comprehensive system in the form of a national catalogue of vocational certifications. The present three systems —state certifications, accredited ones *(titres homologués)* and vocational qualification certificates *(certificats de qualifications professionnelles, CQP)*— will be eligible for registration in this national catalogue. A national commission for vocational qualifications will manage the system and will also set up a new system of qualification levels.

To simplify matters, we applied two criteria against which the selection of frameworks for classifying qualifications can be studied:

(a) a focus on systems incorporating qualifications that are (also) used to denote the results (and the achieved goals) of vocational education at national level;

(b) a focus on all levels identified in vocational education, from pre-vocational training and crafts training to technical and higher vocational education, including university education.

When analysing and comparing classification frameworks, it is important that a number of concepts are accurately defined. The following definitions are used for this report. A 'standard' defines the outcome of a learning/experience process. A standard reflects what the (future) employee/professional must know and be able to apply in professional practice, as laid down in documents and recognised by public authorities and/or social partners. Standards can be stipulated in awards, exit qualifications, certificates, diplomas or other evidence of a study programme. This is the case in Spain, France, Germany and the Netherlands). Standards can also be geared to assessing someone's work or practical experience (England) (4).

A 'unit' is defined as one of a series of components (modules) of a course or training programme that entitle the person in question to a certificate provided these are formally recognised by competent bodies. While modules might be defined by schools or training providers to structure a particular course, units are formally recognised and awarded components.

---

(4) It should be noted that the word 'standard' might be interpreted slightly differently in the various countries. In England and Wales and in the Netherlands, a standard is regarded as a statement concerning a specific competence. In France and Spain, a standard is regarded more as a comprehensive set of competences. This difference should be noted while reading this report.

A 'qualification' is defined as a formal recognition of a standard or a set of standards expressed by a certificate, diploma or other evidence. It is delivered when it has been made clear, through an assessment process, that standards are achieved. A qualification indicates that a person acquired a certificate, either through work experience or after having successfully completed a course or programme, entitling this person to obtain a diploma or some other form of official recognition of value to the labour market or to further education.

1.2. Research method and approach

The research was undertaken in three phases. In the first phase, the national classification frameworks were identified using a common format (see Annex 2). The format focused on the history of the development of the frameworks, the definition of standards as applied by each country, the procedures for developing and approving the standards, and the number of, and definition for, the levels used in the system. National systems were studied in greater detail in two case studies. Two sectors were selected for these case studies: the building sector and the healthcare sector. Apart from shedding light on the problematic use of level criteria in England and Wales and in the Netherlands, the case studies provided no relevant information for the three fields to be covered in the synthesis report. Therefore, there are no specific references to these case studies in this report.

The similarities and differences between national systems and the European five-level training structure were described, as well as the extent to which this almost 20-year-old classification system is still applied. ISCED-97 served as an additional frame of reference ([5]).

This first phase resulted in seven reports: six national studies (Germany (two studies), France, Spain, England and Wales and the Netherlands) and a study on qualification-level developments in tertiary education.

In the second phase, the similarities and differences between national structures and classification systems were analysed at a two-day conference, during which the aspects below were paid particular attention:

(a) the number and description of levels in the respective frameworks for the classification of qualifications and the implicit and/or explicit criteria used for the definition of levels and their characteristics;

---

[5] *International standard classification of education 1997*, Unesco, Paris, 1997; *Classifying educational programmes, manual for ISCED-97 implementation in OECD countries*, OECD, Paris, 1999.

(b) the description of pathways by which a person can acquire a qualification;

(c) the position of standards within the continuum of vocational education provisions, on the one hand, and within employment and occupational hierarchies, on the other: they could be formulated in occupational or educational terms or in relevance for entrance to certain jobs or professional positions;

(d) the mechanisms and procedures for the development of standards, new occupations and professions formulated as training objectives;

(e) the implicit and explicit criteria used for the definition of units and qualifications.

The results of this analysis form the main basis of this report. A draft version was presented to the authors of the individual studies and the conclusions were discussed during the third and last phase of the study. Bibliographical details concerning this report and the six reports prepared by the partner institutes are included in Annex 1.

Anneke Westerhuis
CINOP

2. The scope of national qualification frameworks

The structures included in the study vary in terms of definition and scope between the five Member States. The following picture emerges when these differences are described in greater detail. With the national qualifications framework designed by Sir Ron Dearing, England, Northern Ireland and Wales use a common descriptive structure covering all general, vocational, and occupational qualifications ([6]). It is designed as a framework to which qualifications are submitted for government approval, and for eligibility for use in government-funded education and training. However, qualifications continue to exist outside this system; various kinds of regional or local, sector-specific, company-specific qualifications, and/or international qualifications can be used and attained by learners and candidates.

Such an all-encompassing framework is now being developed and might be implemented in Spain. Because the new framework is not yet in operation, the current Spanish vocational education systems will be regarded as a national framework in Spain in this report. The current Spanish VET structure is similar to the current French one, though with far fewer levels. In fact, Spain has three education subsystems. Two two-level subsystems respectively cover initial VET education and occupational training provided by the Spanish Office for Employment. Strictly speaking, university-based tertiary education can be regarded as a third qualification subsystem.

Since the 1960s, France has used a system of national diplomas for initial vocational and technical education and training programmes and courses. They are classified by levels of attainment and prepare young people for corresponding levels in occupations and professions. This structure is used in parallel as a frame of reference for the *homologation* ([7]) of other forms of (adult or further) education and training and study programmes that are not part of the initial education system. Each training provider can ask for his/her certificates or diplomas to be 'homologated'. This is the case, for instance, with the labour market training activities of the Ministry of Labour. France is planning reform

---

([6]) Dearing, R., *The review of qualifications for 16-19-year-olds*, 1996.
([7]) The French term *homologation* refers to the process by which a certificate is accredited as equivalent to a national diploma.

on the same lines as Spain: the introduction of a framework encompassing existing ones.

The Netherlands has two frameworks closely connected to secondary vocational education and to higher professional education. The (new) classification framework for secondary vocational education is particularly intended to be used for the certification of different kinds of prior learning and work experience.

Germany has no comprehensive-level framework classifying vocational qualifications. Different classification systems exist for the various types of vocational education and training (initial education, advanced training), and different classification criteria may apply at appropriate levels within each of the different education and training sectors/segments (healthcare, building and construction, engineering, crafts and commercial occupations, etc.).

2.1. Germany

Germany does not have a comprehensive system for the classification of qualifications. Its standards and qualifications, which include vocational and professional education, are the nearest to such a system. This type of education can be divided into five subsystems and three levels. The exit qualifications of the educational curricula and training programmes or the examination regulations of the subsystems can be regarded as qualifications. These comprise qualifications set for educational programmes geared to the *anerkannte Ausbildungsberufe, Schulberufe* or *Assistentenberufe* (to be classified at ISCED level 3) (8) and for the national and federal state level regulated *Weiterbildungsberufe* (ISCED level 4). The awards provided by schools for higher vocational education can also be interpreted as qualifications (ISCED level 5). A characteristic of Germany is that, besides this hierarchy of qualifications in levels, it is possible to identify a horizontal dimension in terms of educational fields regulated by the national State (*Bund*) and the federal states *(Länder)*. Both the national State and the federal states can regulate ISCED level 3 and 4 qualifications. Vertical relationships between subsystems are stronger than horizontal relationships, especially in the case of one organisation (ministry) responsible for qualifications at the second-level subsystem. All subsystems, except qualifications regulated by the chambers, are included in this report.

---

(8) The *Ausbildungsberufe* subsystem is dominant at the third level, providing 90% of the qualifications.

Table 1. **German vocational and professional education subsystems and levels**

Qualifications regulated at national level	Qualifications regulated by the federal states
1. Ausbildungsberufe (ISCED level 3)	2. Schulberufe (ISCED level 3)
3. Weiterbildungsberufe (ISCED level 4)	4. Weiterbildungsberufe (ISCED level 4)
5. Fach- and Hochschulberufe (ISCED level 5)	

2.2. Spain

Spain is in a transitional phase. In 1999 a new system was introduced. This new system, the national system of qualifications (*sistema nacional de cualificaciones, SNC*), is not yet fully operational. It is expected to become a general reference framework for all standards and qualifications delivered at all levels as well as unifying the current great variety of classification systems of vocational standards. It is also meant to enable the accreditation of units for the assessment of competences of those in work and to provide employment references to increase the transparency of sectoral, regional, national and European labour markets.

The *SNC* could be regarded as a 'supra-system' as it will connect all current qualification systems: the initial VET system provided in schools and colleges, the occupational training courses organised by the Spanish Office of Employment (*Instituto Nacional de Empleo, INEM*), the systems of the so-called autonomous communities (regions) and the system for careers classification. It aims to assume a position at the interface between the education system on the one hand and the labour market on the other.

Due to the fact that the system is not yet fully operational, we have to refer to current systems for the definition of qualifications and classification levels. Three subsystems can be identified in the Spanish education system. Within each subsystem, levels can be differentiated on the basis of the characteristics of professions for which they prepare. Currently, two subsystems can be identified in VET: one for classifying secondary vocational education and one for occupational training provided by *INEM*. In addition, the Spanish education system identifies two types of education at tertiary level: university colleges and advanced technical colleges. The differences between these two types are based on differences between the professions for which they prepare.

Qualifications at tertiary level are considered to be at levels 4 and 5 in the framework of the European five-level structure.

2.3. France

France has a six-level national classification framework in the form of a system of diplomas for initial vocational study programmes. These diplomas cover the standards that apply to all initial vocational education/training. The framework is important as it is used as a frame of reference and as a source of inspiration for systems developed later. Since 1992, the standards of the diplomas/qualifications may also be used for accreditation of (prior) work experience, but there has been little take-up of this procedure. The system also recognises study programmes other than the standard ones delivered outside the formal education system. All kinds of study programmes and courses can be 'homologated' by the *Commission technique d'homologation des titres et diplômes (CTH)*. This commission determines the position of the study programmes in terms of level and of speciality *(spécialité)*.

In parallel, a number of business and industrial sectors have developed their own system of accreditation using certificates of professional qualifications *(certificats de qualifications professionnelles, CQP)*. Each *CQP* has set up its own standards and does not provide for processes of accreditation of prior experiences. Only a few *CQP* have been presented for homologation.

Currently, France, at the initiative of the State Secretary for Vocational Education, is considering a cohesive, comprehensive system partly merging, though definitely linking together, existing ones. It will act as a national and sectoral reference for all existing certifications, standardising their references to expected competences and abilities. This new system will introduce the potential for certification through the accreditation of prior experience and personal learning *(acquis personnels et professionnels)*.

2.4. The Netherlands

The Netherlands has two subsystems for classifying vocational qualifications. A new classification system for the qualifications offered in secondary vocational education came into operation in 1997. It has four levels and is intended to be used for the accreditation of prior learning and work experience as well. Inspired by the national vocational qualification (NVQ) concept, qualifications and curricula for initial vocational education are uncoupled. To what extent this uncoupling of the classification system of qualifications and standards from initial vocational education programmes has managed to succeed is discussed below.

The second system includes qualifications in higher professional education. In the eyes of secondary vocational education, higher professional education is labelled as level 5. Higher professional education itself seldom uses this label, as it regards itself as a part of higher education ([9]). Programmes to prepare for key competences were introduced in higher professional education in 1997. Institutes for higher professional education agreed to define school-based curricula according to national professional profiles and a common 70 % curriculum. In this report, the attainment goals included in these curricula will be regarded as qualifications ([10]).

These two classifications do not together cover the entire field of vocational and professional education programmes and training courses. The two systems are not exclusive, as they do not classify the certificates (qualifications) of the many study programmes and training courses for the working population (post-initial or continuing vocational education). In addition, university-level education has its own internal classification system.

2.5. United Kingdom (England and Wales)

It is important to recognise the status of the national framework for qualifications in England. The framework of five levels and three types of qualifications (general, vocational and occupational qualifications) is used as a common descriptive framework by the regulatory bodies in England, Wales and Northern Ireland. Scotland operates a different system of qualifications, although there are equivalence agreements in each specific case for SVQs (Scotland) and NVQs.

The requirement in law is that qualifications have to be approved by the regulatory body [the QCA in England (the Qualifications and Curriculum Authority); the ACAC in Wales (the *Awdurdof Cwricwlwm ac Asesu Cymru*) and the CCEA for Northern Ireland (the Council for the Curriculum, Examinations and Assessment)] for use in publicly funded programmes of education and training.

([9]) According to Dutch laws, institutes for higher professional education and universities together form higher education (*hoger onderwijs*).

([10]) Is higher professional education preparing for level 5 qualifications or is it part of an implicit structure of higher or tertiary education, which also includes university levels? We come back to this somewhat ambiguous position of higher professional education in Section 8.

This includes pre-16 education, further education, and government-funded training programmes.

The framework is potentially all-inclusive, since all qualifications can notionally be fitted into it. However, qualifications are only related to the framework in any formal way if they are submitted to the regulatory body for approval (the QCA in England), and while all qualifications for use in schools are submitted, not all vocational qualifications are government-funded, and thus not all are submitted to the QCA.

NVQs (national vocational qualifications) fit into the third part of the national framework – as occupational qualifications. NVQs are based on sets of standards drawn up by industry bodies and are approved by the QCA, using specific criteria. NVQs are designed principally for use in the workplace (to certificate the results of training/learning, or to recognise prior achievement). They are used to a considerable degree in colleges of further education, and to a very limited extent in schools. NVQs currently account for approximately 50% of the occupational qualifications awarded in England; other qualifications from a very wide range of bodies make up the remainder. These are referred to in official statistics as 'non-NVQ vocational qualifications'.

NVQs and GNVQs (general national vocational qualifications) are the main instrument for government policy in respect of rationalising the system of vocational qualifications. They aim to reduce the numbers of competing/overlapping qualifications and introduce new qualifications in areas where there are gaps in provision. However, the national qualifications framework can accommodate non-NVQ vocational qualifications, and the policy is shifting towards admitting more of these to sit alongside NVQs.

The original policy intention (1986) for NVQs was that they should replace all other vocational qualifications. They included strict criteria relating to the form of the qualifications as well as the requirement for them to be linked to occupational standards. By the late 1990s, this original intention had been moderated. The requirement to link the qualifications to occupational standards was retained, but the original stringent requirements on the form of the qualifications were relaxed. This represents a move from an exclusive framework to an inclusive framework, which admits a higher proportion of the vocational qualifications, but continues to ensure that they are based on occupational standards.

2.6. Summary

The scope of a classification system for qualifications can be described using three criteria:
- (a) whether or not the application and use of the system is broader than purely for the identification and regulation of curricula and diplomas of formal vocational education and training programmes;
- (b) whether or not a system is a comprehensive framework, incorporating qualifications of different levels while these levels are defined in a coherent way;
- (c) whether or not the system is monopolistic in the sense of comprising all obtainable qualifications and that no other system is being used.

None of the systems presented in this report meets all three criteria. None of the countries has a classification system consisting of one unique set of qualifications serving as the reference frame to certify a wide variety of learning and work experience at a wide and exhaustive range of levels. At the moment ,the national system of England and Wales comes closest, but does not meet the last criterion, as a great number of (non-formally recognised) qualifications are not included in the national framework. The reforms now being discussed in Spain and France also come close, but do not meet the third criterion, since anyone will continue to have the freedom to develop and to deliver qualifications. However, this third criterion might never be realised. A completely unified structure does not seem to be very realistic; there will always be organisations or industries that will deliver certificates. This is surely the case for England and Wales and France but also for Germany with certificates delivered by local and regional chambers in further and continuing education and training. Like the national system of England and Wales, French and Spanish reforms are trying to improve connections between already existing frameworks. What society will make of these efforts remains to be seen, especially in terms of recruitment and take-up of training leading to acquisition of qualifications at higher levels.

Only the current English and French multi-level frameworks cover both secondary and tertiary qualifications ([11]). Germany, the Netherlands and Spain have no comprehensive frameworks covering secondary and tertiary qualifications. In all three countries, VET and higher professional education can be regarded as subsystems within the national education system, each having its own sub-levels and procedures for standard setting and qualification devel-

---

([11]) It should be noted, however, that level 4 and 5 NVQs are not widely used in English tertiary education as the universities and schools for higher professional education strongly prefer to develop their own study programmes instead of implementing NVQs.

opment. In fact ,these countries have more formalised qualification frameworks for secondary vocational education and an implicit qualification framework covering tertiary education. Because of this ambiguous position of tertiary qualifications in multi-level frameworks, the project team decided to analyse the definition of levels in tertiary qualifications more deeply in Section 7 of this report.

The following figure represents the current situation.

Figure 1. **The characteristics of current qualification frameworks**

Standards closely linked to
formal vocational education and training

France

Germany

Spain

No comprehensive
and cohesive
system of levels

A comprehensive
system of levels

England and Wales

Netherlands

Standards are not closely linked
to formal vocational education and training

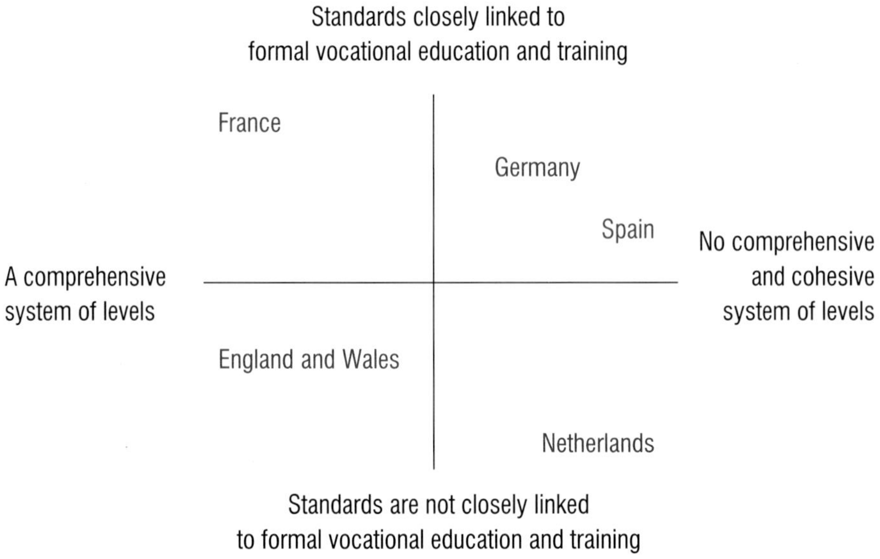

3. The definition of standards

Standards form a link between occupational practice and the competences required by people in occupational practice. They link the characteristics of work in terms of tasks, abilities and skills to the results of learning. In some cases, standards are expressed in terms of contents, certificates and diplomas of formal vocational education and training programmes (Germany and Spain). This link with vocational education and training is less exclusive in France, England and Wales and the Netherlands (¹²).

3.1. Germany

Five subsystems were identified in Germany, all part of the education system. In all subsystems, the learning objectives, linked to supra-institutional curriculum documents or examination regulations in the case of the *Weiterbildungs-* and *Fortbildungsberufe*, can be regarded as standards. The ways in which standards are defined will be identified for each of these subsystems.

The *anerkannten Ausbildungsberufe* (ISCED level 3, national State regulated) are delivered in linked work and training programmes, in apprenticeship or in technical colleges. They all include periods of on-the-job training and are based on clearly defined national exit qualifications comprising general and vocational components of educational programmes. The qualifications are laid down in training regulations (*Ausbildungsordnungen*) in terms of the knowledge and skills to be developed during training. The *Ausbildungsordnungen* also includes training schedule guidance for the providers of training and the time to be spent on training. In addition, curriculum elements for the school component of the education programme are laid down by each federal state (*Land*), on the basis of coordination within the Standing Conference of Education Ministers of the Federal States (*Ständige Konferenz der Kultusminister der Länder, KMK*). Programmes are stipulated as fields of learning and as guidelines for the time to be spent on teaching in each year of training.

The *Assistentenberufe* (ISCED level 3, federal state regulated) are generally taught in full-time school-based education programmes. The standards of

---

(¹²) In the Netherlands, however, this feature is limited to the standards developed for secondary vocational education.

these education programmes are part of the curricula autonomously stipulated by the respective federal states. They are generally based on framework agreements (*Rahmenvereinbarungen*) concluded within the *KMK*. Normally, the curricula for in-company training programmes in all sectors leading to recognised occupations are laid down at national (federal) level. All sectors have various frameworks for the design of supra-institutional curricula, which, however, follow common lines in terms of duration and the combination of on-the-job and off-the-job training.

For example, in the mechanical engineering sector, it is customary that these curricula include a list of skills and competences required by the graduate on completion of training. They also indicate those fields in which such skills are required. There are no other guidelines for the formulation of standards.

Different approaches can be distinguished with the *Weiterbildungsberufe* (ISCED level 4, both national State and federal state regulated). For example, the *Meister* concept is applied at national level in the crafts, industrial and agricultural sectors. The assistant or *Fachwirt* concept applies in commercial trades and in service employment. Only the examination requirements have been laid down in both concepts. An individual is free to decide how his/her knowledge and skills are acquired in preparing for the examination. In addition to the acceptance criteria for an examination, the regulations cover only the subjects that will be examined. For instance, the *Meisterprüfung* in craft and industry comprises managerial skills, technical knowledge and skills, organisational, legal and commercial knowledge, management and personnel and training skills. In the framework of continuing education and training (*Weiterbildung*), vocational education and training programmes are set up by the federal states. They are usually classified into three groups: technicians *(Techniker)* ([13]), business assistants (*Betriebswirte*) and designers (*Gestalter*). The subjects (disciplines) and learning objectives stated in the regulations could be regarded as standards.

In higher professional and university education (ISCED levels 5 and 6), standards are also integrated into the respective study programmes and the respective examination regulations: the university or higher professional diplomas or state exams (*Hochschulabschlüsse*). These are usually developed at faculty level by the teaching staff, taking into account the *Länder*-specific regulations and legislation. However, they are normally based on:

(a) formats and framework agreements developed by the Federal Science Council (*Wissenschaftsrat*) in close cooperation with the *KMK* and the faculties;

([13]) Technicians are trained in full-time technical colleges after having passed through initial training.

(b) the federal framework law for higher education (*Hochschulrahmenge-setz*) that is implemented by federal state specific laws on higher educa-tion (*Hochschulgesetze*).

Although developments are moving towards a more practical focus, special-isation and knowledge-oriented design still dominate curricula and examina-tions, i.e. standards.

3.2. Spain

The new national classification system of vocational standards (*SNC*) aims to establish a coherent framework for the current large variety of qualifications, standards and different classification systems. Current qualifications include the catalogue of regulated vocational training qualifications (for initial voca-tional education) and the compendium of professional proficiency certificates (training provisions offered by the Office of Employment). They can be regarded as standards. As the *SNC* has not yet been implemented, we will focus the analysis of the definition of standards on the current *MEC* and *INEM* systems representing the standards for initial vocational education and occupational training.

The *MEC* regards educational goals as standards [14]. Defined with evalu-ation by the education system in mind, they are identified within a so-called professional profile. A professional profile consists of a series of actions and results being the expected and may include the conduct of people in the respec-tive work situation or organisation, in fact professional competences. The basic value of these professional competences is twofold: while they are applicable to all the sector's productive organisations that have similar production targets, relevant and significant skills are deduced from these on which, in turn, educa-tion and training programmes or curricula are based.

Each professional competence includes a series of performance criteria determining the desired level of achievement and providing a precise refer-ence for the evaluation of work in a given productive context. They also act as a guideline for the evaluation of professional skills and knowledge in education/training centres.

A professional competence includes all factors making up the professional performance and qualification. These factors can be summarised as follows:

---

[14] These goals are, in effect, educational criteria for assessment and evaluation indicating a person is able to perform the activity associated with the vocational standard at an acceptable level of perform-ance.

(a) technical skills: skills to operate effectively on the (material and immaterial) objects and variables that intervene directly in the fabrication or delivery of the product or service;

(b) organisational and economic skills: skills to coordinate the various activities, to organise rationally, technical, social and economic aspects, as well as to perform more general tasks linked with the profession;

(c) environmental cooperation and relationship skills: skills permitting response to the determining factors of relations and procedures established in the organisation of work related to the profession, plus efficient integration, whether horizontally or vertically, cooperating socially and productively with other workers;

(d) troubleshooting skills: the skills necessary to respond to problems, breakdowns or faults detected in procedures, established sequences, equipment, systems, products and/or services related to the profession.

3.3. France

The methodology for defining French standards for formal vocational diplomas in initial education, extensively elaborated by the Ministry of Education, is presented below. However, most of the other ministries delivering national certifications (for initial or further qualifications) manage similar processes (labour, agriculture, youth and sport).

The diplomas of the Ministry of Education are specified in three related documents:

(a) an occupational activity frame of reference, describing an individual's activities in an occupational context in terms of goals, conditions and production methods (the description of the occupation);

(b) a certification frame of reference for the occupational field, a regulatory document describing the skills to be attained in that field. A diploma is awarded to confirm these skills; the document specifies the conditions and assessment indicators for the skills;

(c) the examination regulations that prescribe methods and procedures for accrediting and validating skills.

The certification frame of reference and the examination regulations are legally binding and condition the award of a diploma or certificate. The occupational activity frame of reference is not a binding prescription as such. It is understood that its recommendations are integrated into both the certification frame of reference and the examination regulations related to it. The certification frame of reference (*référentiel de certification*) for an occupational field comprises five elements:

(a) a table that relates the occupational activity frame of reference and the certification frame of reference in the given occupational field;

(b) a skills summary which is the counterpart to the definition of activities;

(c) a description of competences and know-how, which specifies what the trained person should be capable of, the conditions of implementation (the available resources and elements of the environment) and the evaluation criteria (the expected performance of the candidate);

(d) a table of relationships between the individual's know-how and associated knowledge;

(e) specifications for associated knowledge, describing the ideas and concepts involved and the limits of knowledge required for the exams.

The examination regulations (*règlements d'examen*) define the tests. Each test is modelled according to the skills that it assesses, the associated knowledge that it validates, the medium by which it is organised and the nature of the performances expected of the candidate.

The forthcoming reform anticipates that each certification will be included in the national catalogue, and will adopt the methodology of the frame of references described above. Also, it will request that decisions about such certification be taken in the framework of consultative commissions in which social partners are present.

3.4. The Netherlands

The format for the classification of qualifications in secondary vocational education introduced by the Ministry of Education, Culture and Sciences in 1997 is part of the new legislation for secondary vocational education. As in France, Dutch standards are not intended exclusively for secondary vocational education certification, but also for assessment of prior learning and work experience. This option, however, is only weakly stated in official documents. The 1997 Act on Vocational and Adult Education refers to exit qualifications (standards) in terms of knowledge, insight, skills, and in certain cases, the professional attitude required by those completing the education/training programme. This wording is identical to formulations used to define educational goals. In effect, standards are formulated in a school/curriculum terminology.

The publication *Guidelines for the formulation of exit qualifications* ([15]) offers detailed suggestions for the definition of standards. According to these guidelines, standards have to be based on job descriptions: a description of the most

---

([15]) Streumer, W., et al., *Richtlijnen voor het formuleren van eindtermen*, CINOP, 's-Hertogenbosch, 1996.

relevant tasks and activities in an occupation. In fact, occupational tasks and activities are rephrased as the discernible results, choices and decisions made during the execution of activities. They will form the foundation for the competences to be learned at school and in practice. Professional attitudes are regarded as the way in which professional activities are performed; it is commonly understood that these are best acquired in practice during on-the-job training and not at school.

Standards in higher professional education are part of school-based curricula. A group of professionals and experts is invited by schools to produce a profile for the respective profession. Schools cooperate in developing a so-called educational profile covering about 4 720 out of the 6 720 study hours a course in higher professional education will comprise. The learning objectives included in these curricula can be regarded as standards.

3.5. United Kingdom (England and Wales)

National standards aim to describe occupational and/or professional competences in the broadest possible sense, not a competence in a given job role at a particular location. More especially, they do not describe the way in which tasks are completed by a specific individual or the required knowledge and skills in specific work systems. With a focus on outcomes-based occupational competences, national standards are oriented mainly towards sector standards and are derived from in-depth analysis of enterprise requirements. The principal objective is that the standards should relate to occupational competence rather than to the requirements of specific training and vocational education programmes, or to narrow job functions.

The following concepts are included in descriptions of competences:
  (a) 'element', describing the area of competence;
  (b) a 'unit' would typically include between three and eight elements;
  (c) 'performance criteria' describe the outcomes from which a judgment of competence can be made;
  (d) 'range', describing different aspects of the job function, contexts, etc., where competences should be demonstrated;
  (e) 'evidence requirements', stating the type of evidence which should be used as the basis of the assessment of competence;
  (f) 'underpinning knowledge/knowledge requirements', listing the knowledge, principles, theory, etc., related to the area of competence described in the element.

English standards can in no way be regarded as curriculum specifications which would enable a more extensive use of the standards. The present standards leave educationalists, teachers and trainers to translate these into curricula and training programmes – a demanding task – with individual interpretations placing a significant burden on quality assurance arrangements. The intended use of NVQs for accreditation of prior learning is clear (although the practice has proved burdensome for candidates and trainers), but the means by which they can be used in structuring effective learning programmes is considerably more problematic.

3.6. Summary

Standards linked to the educational or training domain were identified in four countries. In Germany and Spain, standards are incorporated into curricula or diplomas. French and Dutch standards are at a somewhat greater distance from vocational education as these standards should also be applicable for the accreditation of prior learning and work experiences. In practice, however, standards are not used extensively for this purpose, especially where the definition of standards tends to be education based (the Netherlands).

The new Spanish system includes a unified set of standards. The *SNC* will coordinate the development of standards for initial vocational education and for the training courses for job-seekers and will establish multipurpose job descriptions. Although these standards seem to be similar to the English NVQ standards, they are, however, intended mainly as exit qualifications for initial and continuing vocational education and training.

The English definition of standards is completely unrelated to formal education or training in schools, colleges or training centres. The original approach to the definition of NVQs – as competence-based, open access qualifications – attempted deliberately to break the link between the results to be achieved and the form of the learning leading to those results [16]. However, in leaving all curriculum development (other than specifying the content to be achieved) to trainers, teachers and those responsible for managing learning

---

[16] 'In systems of education and training where standards of performance are not independently defined, the only concept of a standard is that which is defined by, and imbedded within, the exams or tests set. Assessment is then inevitably tied to such exams and tests. But once standards are set out independently of assessment, as in NVQs, it creates opportunities for different forms of assessment. Instead of allowing the assessment to define the standards, the standards now define what needs to be assessed ' (G. Jessup, *Outcomes: NVQs and the emerging model of education and training,* Falmer, 1991).

and/or assessment, the qualifications provided far less support for structuring effective learning programmes than many policy-makers imagined. The problems that this caused – not least for quality assurance of both learning and assessment– have been recognised. The QCA is now forming a training policy forum, designed to stimulate a more productive relationship between the qualification approval and curriculum development processes.

What characteristics of work should have priority in standards:
(a) specific job requirements or requirements of an occupation, an occupational field or a sector?
(b) current requirements of a given job or occupation, or requirements expected to be relevant in the future?

Everywhere, standards try to compromise between these options. Most standards are supposed to cover personal work experience acquired (or to be obtained) in work settings. At the same time, standards are supposed to support improvement in (raise, broaden, prepare for the future) the competences of learning and working individuals. This is particularly so for courses organised partly at school and partly in professional practice where there is a tension between the opportunity for on-the-job training offered by companies and the need to include future-oriented and more general competences in a programme.

4. The definition of qualifications

What does a qualification say about somebody? What are qualifications meant to say? A qualification is a formal recognition of a standard or a set of standards expressed by a certificate, diploma or other evidence. It is delivered when it has been made clear through an assessment process that standards are achieved. In general, a vocational qualification indicates competence in performing an occupation satisfactorily – to be more precise, satisfactorily in the eyes of those who validated the qualification. Qualifications express the stakeholders' vision as to how and with which competences a person should be equipped for the labour market.

In England and Wales, an NVQ represents the requirements of occupational practice. Like English national standards, an NVQ expresses occupational competences not exclusively linked to vocational education. In the other countries, qualifications are more or less linked to formal vocational education programmes and are exclusively obtainable through educational pathways. Consequently, progression through qualification levels is only possible by taking the education route, perhaps not in theory but most certainly in practice.

4.1. The division of qualifications into units

In three of the five countries, qualifications are divided into units. This means that it is possible to have a part of a full qualification certified. This is the case in England and Wales, the Netherlands and France. In this perspective, it is less relevant whether or not a study programme is structured in modules, but whether there is an opportunity to accredit parts or units of a qualification acquired either by means of full-time study or during, and combined with, work experience. In Germany and Spain, there seems to be a growing interest in designing qualifications by units. However, in Germany, the *Beruf* concept is closely linked to a fully recognised occupational qualification delivered via formal initial or further training. Within continuing education and training, at the interface between initial and further training, however, this unitisation is being introduced more and more ([17]).

([17]) See also the study launched within the Ciretoq network in 1998 on additional qualifications. Publication of this study is forthcoming as a Cedefop reference document.

Unit certification does not automatically mean that these unit certificates have a currency in the labour market. This seems to be the case in England and Wales only. French units are only used to design learner-friendly progression routes through the education system. In France, one can accumulate units up to a full qualification; units are assessed and one obtains a certificate, but these certificates only have value in the framework of a full qualification. In the Netherlands, the situation is somewhat ambiguous. On the one hand, Dutch units serve the same purpose as the French ones, and, on the other hand, Dutch units are regarded as a last resort for young learners in secondary vocational education not willing or wanting to obtain a full qualification.

4.1.1. Germany

As yet, it is not possible in Germany to complete a study programme (any study programme) by acquiring unit-based certificates over a period of time ([18]). This is strongly opposed for the *Ausbildungsberufe*, understandably as in Germany an *Ausbildungsberuf* represents more than a specific vocational education qualification. This qualification has a broader socioeconomic and cultural meaning. Salary structures and rights to social and/or unemployment benefits are connected with the respective vocational qualification. Individuals derive their personal identity from a profession. In addition, trade unions, in particular attach a great deal of importance to the fact that employees' interests remain identical. Their membership comprises mainly those obtaining a recognised vocational education qualification within the dual system of training. The development of units, which could be accredited as parts of a course for an *Ausbildungsberuf*, must be prevented, in their opinion, as it undermines the concept of full qualification.

4.1.2. Spain

In Spain, education programmes are structured in modules designed from the view of professional practice. These modules are not yet certifiable. Using the definitions in this report, the current modules cannot be regarded as units. Since Spanish professional profiles are regarded as having a wider scope than in other countries, discussion is beginning to focus on whether or not to cut these profiles into smaller units.

([18]) In Germany, a number of restricted pilot experiments are being run in this area. Although the concept of dividing programmes into units is disputed within the *Ausbildungsberufe*, continuing education and training are increasingly organised as modular programmes.

4.1.3. **France**

As the need for adult training has grown in France and lifelong training has been encouraged, examination regulations have been adapted. It is now possible to acquire full certification over time by certification of units, the *unités capitalisables*. However, units are not accredited but can be totalled up to reach a full diploma. Without the full process, there is no accreditation: units are of no value on their own.

Another form of working with units is found in the procedures for the accreditation of prior learning and work experience (*validation des acquis professionnels*). This is a way of recognising the value of work in competence building through certification. A candidate receives parts of the certificate in equivalence, meaning that he/she does not need to attend the corresponding parts of education programmes or to take particular tests. However, at least one examination must be taken in one subject.

4.1.4. **The Netherlands**

Units were introduced in the Netherlands to create efficient educational tracks in vocational education, and higher professional education. In higher professional education students are even stimulated to compose their own qualification programme by making their own selection from units offered by different sectors of their own institute or other national or foreign institutes.

Successful completion of a unit entitles the learner to a certificate. If somebody leaves a study programme prematurely, which happens frequently, he or she still has one or more certificates and may later attain one or more certificates. The opposite also applies. If someone wants to register for a study programme, previous certificates can be taken into account or awarded on the basis of prior learning and work experience. The latter approach is new and still being developed. The reasons for the growing interest in this option are the same as in France. As in France, one does not get a full qualification (diploma) until all units are passed successfully.

4.1.5. **United Kingdom (England and Wales)**

In England, there is a tendency towards increasing flexibility in the education and training system by using modular/unit-based structures or breaking qualifications into smaller parts. A significant trend in NVQs is the increasing use by employers and learners of individual units. This fits in with changing skill requirements in work, and with trends towards shorter periods of training whilst working (including learning in the evenings and other non-contracted time) rather than protracted training leading to full qualification. 'Units have a particular significance within the NVQ system because they are independently recognised and certificated. They are like "mini qualifications". A unit should be made up of a coherent group of elements, which together are required to perform an employment function. It is a matter of judgment as to the size of employment function, which is chosen as a unit. It should be large enough to be worthy of separate recognition for a formal credit, that is a competence that would be valued by employers in the context of the occupation in which it is to be practised. On the other hand, it should not be too large. The accumulation of unit credits provides effective motivation for those undergoing programmes of learning...' [19].

Full NVQs are oriented towards occupational competence, and include components relating to future requirements as well as current requirements of work in an occupational area. The focus is thus broader than competence as a narrow job function. The increasing concentration on units rather than full qualifications reflects the perceived needs of learners and employers who are not motivated to work towards broader occupational competence, but seek certification in relation to specific job functions. Whether this rather short-term thinking is sustainable enough in the long term is yet to be seen. The introduction of the so-called new apprenticeships and new training provisions at colleges seems a reversal, offering (new kinds of) full qualifications.

4.1.6. **Summary**

A classification system for qualifications becomes more flexible if the qualifications are divided into units and able to respond to a greater variation in users' requirements. As yet, it is not possible to attain a qualification by the certification of units obtained either by following a training course or by the accreditation of prior learning in Germany and Spain.

The certification of units has advantages of flexibility with regard to individual training needs. These advantages are recognised in all the countries, although not all of them have implemented the unitisation of qualifications. Apart from England and Wales, there is no move towards unitisation in terms of giving labour market currency to units; there is still commitment to full qualification by all key players. National stakeholders, in particular, are fully aware of the temptation offered by unit certification for individual employers and young learners. In Germany, for instance, there is a feeling that the all-or-nothing situation will ultimately result in greater numbers of fully qualified people than an education policy focusing on unitisation. Also, because of the traditional links between qualification and salary system, unitisation would have a major impact on German labour relations.

---

[19] Jessup, G., *Outcomes: NVQs and the emerging model of education and training,* Falmer, 1991.

Unitisation or unit certification of qualifications is a very powerful instrument for lifelong learning, as units can be used by learners to assess the output of learning and working experiences and to design their individual learning and work experience pathways over a longer period of time. In this perspective, unitisation could have an impact on classification frameworks, serving as a frame of reference for individuals and/or companies wanting to assess the currency of working and learning experiences and training courses in smaller units than full qualifications.

4.2. The breadth of a qualification

It is interesting to note that in some countries the breadth of vocational quali- fications is the subject of debate in the sense that the demand for broader qualifications is increasing. In England, for instance, more young people are tending to stay in education for a longer period of time and are deferring choices that limit their options. For example, almost all the growth in qualifications held by 16-19–year-olds (13 % over the period 1991-96) can be allocated to the growth in academic qualifications. Vocational qualifications in this same segment grew by just over 1 %. For its part, the government recognises the importance of general qualifications in the face of increasing change in society and work systems. Finally, employers also recognise this increase in the pace of change and increasingly look for candidates' ability in skills such as communication and team working, as well as requiring specific knowledge and skills relating to current job requirements.

A qualification must represent a larger range of functions than in the past, either to promote the broader deployment of the holders of a qualification, or as a result of the merger of work tasks which were formerly divided over a range of different jobs. Who decides about the breadth of vocational qualifi- cations? As we will see, agreements on the breadth can be reached by those directly involved in the development of (new) qualifications or by stipulating such agreements in central government directives and legislation.

4.2.1. Germany
The German Vocational Training Act stipulates that the *Ausbildungsberufe* are only recognised if they meet the criterion that 'a sufficient demand for the corre- sponding occupations and skills' exists. These skills are to be of enduring validity and not specific to any particular company. Determining the breadth of an *Ausbildungsberuf* is therefore one of the main tasks of the (temporary) commission when developing a new training regulation (*Ausbildungsordnung*).

An *Ausbildungsberuf* is a construct taking into account different needs and objectives. For instance, it should cover a variety of occupations enlarging to the potential for finding a job. As in France, it is not only developments in professional practice but also the opinions of the social partners concerning the optimum starting position for a professional career that are decisive elements in the debate on the breadth of this type of qualification.

Information about developments towards broader definitions of *Schulberufe* and *Weiterbildungsberufe* is not available. A wide range of organisations, public and private bodies, chambers of crafts and/or commerce and federal states are involved. In general, it might be said that the breadth of these qualifications is related to whether or not they are supposed to prepare for a single occupation or a great variety. However, *Schulberufe* and *Assistentenberufe* are generally broader in terms of the range of cognitive know-how and knowledge delivered than the *Ausbildungsberufe*. *Weiterbildungsberufe* may be either specific or broad in nature.

4.2.2. Spain
The Ministry of Education and Culture (MEC) regards vocational standards as indicators for the potential of people to meet existing and future job requirements. As a consequence, vocational qualifications incorporate a broad concept of professional competence.

The *MEC*, through the definition of achievement goals [20] for competence units (defined with their evaluation by the education system in mind), selects the most significant ones in defining professional profiles. These professional profiles are classified according to the professional and educational levels laid down in the 1990 law on the general regulation of the education system (*Ley de Ordenación General del Sistema Educativo, LOGSE*). These correspond to levels 2 and 3 of the European five-level classification system in the directive 'Comparability of vocational training qualifications between European Union Member States' [21]. In this way, the breadth of Spanish qualifications is, in fact, defined by the Ministry of Education and Culture following consultation with tripartite bodies that were established in the same law.

From this perspective, it is interesting to note that the breadth of qualifications is an important point in the debate on the new *SNC*. With regard to the definitions of qualifications, the ideas of the Ministry of Education and Culture and the Ministry of Labour still diverge.

---

[20] Educational criteria of assessment/evaluation indicating a person is able to perform the activity associated with the vocational standard at an acceptable level in a given occupation.

[21] *Ley Orgánica 1/1990* of 3 October of the *Ordenación General del Sistema Educativo* (BOE, 4.10.1990).

4.2.3. **France**

The debate on the breadth of qualifications in France at the moment interprets breadth as transversality. The French Ministry of Education is currently promoting this transversality and breadth of qualifications as an important aim. However, this aim is not always shared by employers' organisations. There are recurrent conflicts with certain representatives on this issue, though not with all of them. The underlying debate revolves around what should be represented within a given qualification. Often, in the consultative commissions put in place by the Ministry of Education, it is not so much developments in occupational practice which are decisive, but the opinions of parties involved in the consultation concerning the optimum starting position for a professional career. Qualifications are social constructs and as such they are bargained between the key players of each sector individually ([22]).

A common characteristic of French certificates (diplomas) is that they are defined by the education or training qualification ([23]) that they award and the specialisation for which the individual receives recognition. Some of these certifications are closely linked to the organisation dispensing the training. Higher education engineering diplomas, for instance, are school-specific or university diplomas, which are linked to the accrediting university. As a consequence, the debate on the breadth of qualifications is a debate on the breadth of the various certificates or diplomas. This leads to different outcomes. For example, France has experienced a big reduction in numbers of *CAP*, while, at the same time, the breadth of *CAP* standards has increased. In contrast, the *BTS* have increased in number, but not in breadth. The *DUT* qualifications have remained stable.

4.2.4. **The Netherlands**

The Netherlands appears to conduct a somewhat dualistic policy. On the one hand, the 1997 Act on Vocational Education stipulates that a qualification must be based on one or more broad, future-oriented occupational profiles. These profiles are elaborated in close consultation with the social partners of the sector in question and must be validated by them. As a result, the ultimate definition of the breadth of the qualification is left to the social partners, as is the case in the German *Ausbildungsberufe* (occupations in which formal training takes place*)*.

---

[22] See Heinz, W. R., in Cedefop (Sellin, B)., *European trends in the development of occupations and qualifications*, Volume II, Thessaloniki, 1999 , p. 15.

[23] The main diploma titles are the *CAP* (certificate of vocational education), the *BEP* (vocational studies diploma), the *baccalaureate*, the *BTS* (higher technical diploma), the *DUT* (university technology diploma), the engineering diploma, the licence, the master's, the *DEA* (advanced studies diploma), the *DESS* (higher specialised studies) and the doctorate.

However, in contrast to Germany, the Dutch social partners seem to be less convinced of the overall need to increase the breadth of qualifications. One of the main reasons for this need for differentiation is the tendency of social partners to meet the wish of subsectors ('the rank and file') for having their 'own' qualifications. This irritates schools, which are faced with the organisational consequences of such a fragmentation. Of course, this approach also involves a risk for the careers of young people, who are trained in narrow specialisations.

The situation in higher professional education is changing in terms of breadth of qualifications. In 1995, an influential report ([24]) concluded that, due to a policy of attracting as many students as possible, institutes for higher professional education were inclined to introduce a wide range of new qualifications, either focusing on a narrow segment of business and industry or a wide range of job positions. The report found this proliferation of qualifications unacceptable and the cause of much confusion among employers in particular. A process of coordinated curriculum development followed but, in 1999, this policy was dropped again. The new key policy seems to be freedom of choice, answering student wishes. Students are offered the opportunity to compose their own study programme from units offered by their own and other institutes ([25]). Now students will determine the breadth of qualifications .

4.2.5. **United Kingdom (England and Wales)**
One of the objectives of the national English classification system was to rationalise the number of qualifications, ensuring that all levels and sectors were provided with appropriate qualifications, reducing complexity, overlap and duplication, and enabling more effective progression in the system. The national framework (1998) is designed to be inclusive – that is, to include all sectors and levels. The gap-filling exercise has been relatively successful, with qualifications now available in areas previously poorly served – for example, retail and distribution. With these crucial infrastructure revisions, there has been a trend towards a reduction in the numbers of vocational qualifications. This has gathered pace in the last three years. Similarly, the number of non-NVQ vocational qualifications that were included in the crucial government schedule of approved qualifications has dropped significantly.

([24]) Vereniging van Hogescholen, *Niet meer maar beter, verslag van de commissie referentiekader onderwijsaanbod,* The Hague, 1995.

([25]) Ministerie van Onderwijs, Cultuur en Wetenschappen, *Ontwerp Hoger Onderwijs en Onderzoek Plan 2000,* Zoetermeer, 1999.

However, the possibility of increasing the breadth of these recognised qualifications is restricted by the users' requirements of the system. Some employers cite the broadness of the NVQ units as a problem rather than as a benefit, since it requires a candidate to do more than his/her current job in order to obtain certification. In many cases, the response is to interpret the generalised descriptors in the units into the specifics of current jobs, narrowing the description of competence in the process. This variability in the interpretation of NVQs during the assessment process moves the award from occupational competence to job competence.

4.2.6. **Summary**

In the countries examined, social partners and professional organisations are involved in the establishment of the breadth of vocational qualifications. Where the business community has a strong influence on the composition of the qualifications, the breadth of qualifications is notable. This is possibly because the tension between the two functions of a classification system are brought to the fore more obviously. On the one hand, there is a wish to include specific and rather narrow qualifications in the system for the benefit of subsectors, groups of companies and even individual companies. On the other hand, there is a wish to provide those working and studying with a broader (career) perspective than expressed in the current occupational practice.

In short, the debate focuses on whether qualifications must represent the actual professional practice or whether qualifications must be tools for innovating occupational practice, and for the improvement of the prospects of both the working and studying population in their present or future careers.

5. The definition of levels in qualification frameworks

In the previous sections, we have seen that qualifications are related to occupational practices, to vocational education or to both fields. What can be said about levels in the frameworks? Apart from studying the differences between the systems in terms of the number of levels, it is also interesting to observe the way in which levels are defined. Are these levels defined with the features of a traditional education system in mind or are they supposed to represent an occupational hierarchy?

Different approaches are taken. The various German subsystems represent different types of education, having their characteristics in terms of admission requirements, minimum educational achievements, type of subsequent position in the labour market or education/training, goals of the training/learning programmes and the duration of the course. In contrast, the English criteria have been derived from the customary manner in which occupations (work activity) are classified in the business community. The other countries apply a mixed set of criteria: to a certain extent, they want to take into account the differences in the demands of occupations and work environments, while at the same time the criteria are closely linked to the school system.

5.1. Germany

Although Germany has no explicit and comprehensive system for the classification of vocational qualifications, it can be assumed that the *Ausbildungsberufe* and *Schulberufe*, the national State and federal states regulated *Weiterbildungsberufe*, and the *Hochschul-abschlüsse* represent five distinct subsystems at three levels. Relationships between these five subsystems in vocational education become clear when looking at differences in descriptors and the paths to be followed to achieve a qualification in a subsystem.

The training programmes for the *Ausbildungsberufe* (ISCED level 3 [26]) are open to everyone who has completed compulsory general education; no formal

---

[26] As Germany does not have a cohesive classification structure, the ISCED classification system is sometimes used to position the qualifications (school subsystems) as this system is based on input criteria.

qualification is required apart from a school-leaving certificate. The apprentices, however, must succeed in obtaining a training contract with a company ([27]). As a rule, the programme takes three and a half years. The subsequent position in the labour market is labelled as 'skilled worker, skilled employee'. The so-called (*Ausbildungs-) Berufsprinzip*, or the principle of recognised, regulated occupations, is the most important descriptor for this subsystem. It includes ten points, referring both to occupational practice and education characteristics. This principle expresses the German consensus that competence can best be achieved by a mix of study and work, incorporating the following:
   (a) sufficient demand for the corresponding skills, which are to be of enduring validity and not specific to any particular company;
   (b) training for skilled, autonomous, planned, executed and monitored activities in as broad a field as possible;
   (c) gearing towards long-term occupational activity irrespective of age;
   (d) basis for advanced training and occupational advancement;
   (e) acquisition of the ability to reason and act autonomously in applying knowledge and skills.

   Admission to the *Schulberufe* (also classified at ISCED level 3) is more strict. Where no formal qualification is required for the *Ausbildungsberufe*, *Schulberufe* are only open to learners with an intermediate secondary or equivalent education certificate. Compared to a dual-system qualification, the qualification obtained is a 'starter' qualification, although instruction at full-time vocational colleges is geared to developing genuine occupational competence. This is firstly because the courses are shorter (in most cases two years) and secondly because the emphasis is on developing occupational knowledge and general practical skills. Although periods of in-company practical training are mandatory, the genuine occupational competence aspired to is probably not really acquired until the ex-student/pupil gets work experience in employment.

   This qualification, however, does allow for a flexible transition to further education/training provisions within the general education and vocational training system and further on into higher professional education at *Fachhochschulen*. In designing programmes and determining occupational profiles linked to these assistant or technical occupations, there is no involvement of the social partners. No formal procedures exist for involving employers' federations or trade unions in the process of devising the training programmes for these occupations, which are controlled by each regional (*Land*) government.

([27]) Contracts between the trainee and the training provider or company identify the rights and obligations of both sides. These training contracts in parallel are regarded as a specific work/employment contract.

An explicit distinction is made between initial vocational qualifications (*Ausbildungsberufe* and *Schulberufe*) and advanced vocational qualifications (*Weiterbildungs-* or *Fortbildungsberufe*; generally classified at ISCED level 4). Federal and State legal provisions accordingly stipulate that advanced qualifications must be regulated in a way that allows a clear distinction from the respective initial qualification. The higher level of an advanced qualification is also emphasised by the fact that the admission criteria here include a recognised initial qualification plus several years of relevant vocational experience.

At tertiary education level, or in higher professional education, no further formal differentiation is made by level. In practice, differentiations exist between graduates from universities (*wissenschaftliche Hochschulen, Kunsthochschulen* and *Technische Hochschulen*) and other higher education establishments such as *Fachhochschulen*. With regard to hierarchically ranked occupational opportunities and salary scales in the public or intermediate domain, deductions can be made about qualification profiles and, as already described, about levels, depending on the type of university and type of (academic) degree. A particular differentiation exists in Germany's public service having four different careers, clearly depending on the levels of education/training reached by candidates. The placing of graduates from *Fachhochschulen* seems to be problematic. In the private sector, they get access to the highest positions in management or in R & D identical to graduates from scientific universities. This is not the case, however, in the public sector and in areas often following the staff regulations applicable in public services, for example in intermediate and public enterprises, in churches and bigger non-profit-making organisations. Graduates from *Fachhochschulen* are put at a disadvantage as compared to those from universities and other *wissenschaftliche Hochschulen*. Thus, we could question whether or not Germany has four levels of education/training and qualification.

5.2. Spain

Taking into account that specific characteristics of the new national classification system (*SNC*) of vocational qualifications are still under discussion, the current classification system for vocational education is analysed in this section. In the education system, according to the *MEC*, two levels of qualification are defined in vocational education. In fact, there are three levels (levels 1, 2 and 3) but this report concentrates on levels 2 and 3, as level 1 corresponds to social guarantee programmes outside the education system. These two levels are based on:

(a) the nature and context of the work (work processes and procedures, information and inputs, nature and types of decision, scope of relationships, type of organisational relationships);

(b) the skills required to carry out activities in a job/occupation (creativity and innovation, interpretation, initiative and decision-making, training and experience).

The essential and distinguishing features of each level and the criteria that define a level of qualification are listed in Table 2.

Table 2

DESCRIPTORS	NATURE AND CONTEXT OF THE WORK				
	Work processes and procedures	Information and inputs	Nature and types of decisions	Scope of relationships	Type of organisational relationships
Intermediate (level 2)	Formalised	Defined and pre-existing	Alternatives limited to certain resources, tools and rates	Individual and possibly group	They require task control
	Technical variables	Indicative and binding technique: part specifications, instruction manuals, codes		Internal	
Advanced (level 3)	Non-formalised	Totally or partly undefined	They affect procedures, resources and technical efficiency	Group regulated reciprocally	They require supervision of aims
	Technical/ scientific and organisational variables	Technical/ organisational/ economic: general plans, process manuals. Need to process information		Unit External	

Table 2 *(continued)*

DESCRIPTORS	SKILLS, KNOWLEDGE, EXPERIENCE			
	Creativity and innovation	Interpretation	Initiative and decision-making	Training and experience
Intermediate (level 2)	Improve processes and procedures	Understand the process and detect abnormal behaviour in a certain range of values	Operate under limited autonomy and in accordance with established procedures	Compulsory secondary education level
		Assess ambiguous messages		Technical/practical experience
	Find connections between existing concepts	Evaluate the relative importance of several factors of the process	Evaluate suitably and rapidly the contingencies of the process between various alternatives given	Significant abilities and skills
Advanced (level 3)	Create or define processes and procedures	Understand the process and evaluate the consequences of non-codified abnormal behaviour	Operate with full autonomy within the assigned responsibility	Baccalaureate level
				Technical/scientific grounding
	Find connections between existing or new concepts and combine them to produce new results	Discern messages or limited or contradictory information	Evaluate the most suitable and fastest processes and decide on new alternatives	Experience solving technical problems

Source: Ministry of Education and Science, Madrid.

According to the *MEC*, in its White Paper on the reform of the education system (1989), a level 2 qualification must enable people to acquire the knowledge and skills appropriate to a worker skilled in a certain occupation with extensive basic training, plus communication skills and an aptitude for exchanging information flows and participating effectively in teamwork.

A level 3 qualification must enable people to acquire the knowledge and skills appropriate to intermediate technicians with multipurpose training and a general and coordinated view of the system in which they operate (mechanical, electrical, administrative, technical/healthcare, etc.), assessing the function and purpose of the different elements of the respective activities.

5.3. France

The French education and training system is structured according to pathways preparing for general, technical or vocational education certificates (diplomas). The common characteristic shared by these diplomas is that they are defined by the qualification they award and the specialisation for which the accredited individual receives recognition. Some of these diplomas stand out by being fundamentally linked to the organisation dispensing the training. This is the case in higher education with engineering diplomas, for instance, which are school specific or with university diplomas, which are linked to the accrediting university. This explains why there are so many diplomas, several thousands to be exact. In order for them to be comprehensible to the whole of society, it is necessary to have a classification system: a qualification-level structure or classification system ensuring transparency.

The 1969 training-level classification system, presented in this report, was created as part of French economic planning studies and focused on prospective professional recruitment needs for different types of training at various levels. Since the system was initially designed as an economic planning tool, it was used to classify the workforce according to the type of studies pursued and the levels attained, and to help establish education/training policies for young people. Hence, the system's purpose was to express occupations in terms of diplomas by creating a correspondence between the degree of qualification associated with a given job and the required scholastic standards (diploma and duration of studies). It could thus be claimed that the requirements of an occupation were satisfied.

However, translating occupations into diplomas was everything but non-problematic. Translation was easy for one group of occupations, either because the standards of admission and access were known or officially regulated, as in the fields of medicine, professional engineering or the liberal professions, or because occupations were at the bottom of the hierarchy, in service employment for example. Only 30 % of the working population in the 1960s fell into this last group. For the other occupations, it was much harder to define a correspondence and it became necessary to call upon experts who, in turn, relied on work and occupational analyses.

The role of the classification systems in analysing prospective needs should not hide the fact that the State developed this system as a tool for active educational policies directed at standardising education and vocational training provisions and outcomes. The idea was that the use of this classification system should not be confined to policy-making by government agencies and bodies. It should guide labour and management in their recruitment and staff policies, as both parties could easily identify an individual's qualifications. The goal of the system was to enable the State to verify titles and objectives of education/training programme titles that were less well known than national diplomas. For this reason, the adoption of this classification system led to the establishment of a certification and *homologation* commission responsible for positioning all diplomas offered on the system's grid.

The six levels of the classification system classify individuals both by occupations and diplomas, establishing between both a 'normal' equivalence. The levels are defined as:

Levels I and II	Personnel occupying positions, which usually require a level of training equal or superior to the university *licence* or diplomas of schools for professional engineer.
Level III	Personnel occupying positions, which usually require the higher technician diploma or a diploma from the *IUTs* ([28]) or having successfully finished exams at the end of the first cycle of higher education.
Level IV	Personnel occupying supervisory staff positions or possessing a qualification level equivalent to a technical or technician baccalaureate or technician diploma.
Level V	Personnel occupying positions, which usually require a training level equivalent to the *BEP* and the *CAP*.
Level Va	Personnel occupying positions, which require short training lasting no longer than a year, leading, in particular, to the certificat d'éducation professionnelle (certificate of vocational education) or any other equivalent certificate or qualification.
Level VI	Personnel occupying positions, which require no training beyond the end of compulsory education.

([28]) *Instituts universitaires technologiques* (technological university institutes).

The classifying principle is based on the effect of education/training programmes in enhancing social status. From this viewpoint, the classification system embraces a universalistic principle, since it is not attached to training programme conditions but to the objectives of the education/training programmes. It is possible to classify, with the help of a certification commission, all national diplomas according to their respective objectives. This universality does not extend to international compatibility as at each level a wide range of qualifications are classified.

Hence, there was the determination to establish new social standards for evaluating educational investments. The success of this policy has been mixed and depends on which part of the social field is considered. It has partially succeeded in penetrating the French production system. The standards of this classification system were adopted in a number of collective agreements in the manufacturing industry but its application is far from generally accepted when such agreements are negotiated between labour and management.

The policy succeeded more within the education system, given that it guided the educational reforms of the 1960s, which included the extension of compulsory education to the age of 16, the development of vocational *lycées* and schools and the appearance of new diplomas such as the *brevets d'études professionnelles* (vocational studies certificates) or *the diplômes universitaires technologiques* (technical university diplomas). The policy created the situation where it became absolutely normal to rank diplomas independently of specific education/training programmes, whether they were oriented towards general, technical or vocational subjects.

5.4. The Netherlands

The qualification framework for Dutch secondary vocational education comprises four levels. It is usual to allocate higher professional qualifications at level 5. Levels 1 to 4 form a cohesive qualification framework. The levels of this framework are defined in a so-called 'format'. The criteria for the positioning of qualifications in the differing levels are part of this format. Level 5 is not part of this framework, neither is it used in higher professional education for labelling its qualifications. The description of the levels is pinned onto the characteristics of the professional practice for which the qualifications prepare the individual: the boundaries of responsibilities, the complexity (of the work) and the specificity of the required knowledge and skills needed in professional practice.

Level 1, 'assistant', is responsible for his/her own activities. Work consists primarily of the application of automated routines and (to a limited extent) the application of standard procedures. It implies job-related skills and knowledge.

Level 2, 'basic occupational practitioner', is responsible for his/her own activities. In addition, he/she and his/her colleagues share a collective responsibility and cooperate with colleagues. Work consists of applying automated routines and standard procedures. It implies occupation-related skills and knowledge.

Level 3, 'all-round practitioner', is responsible for his/her own activities and should account for his/her actions to his/her colleagues (non-hierarchical). In addition a worker has an explicit and hierarchical responsibility: he/she monitors and supervises the application of automated routines and standard procedures. His/her work comprises the application of standard procedures and combining standard procedures. In addition, he/she combines or devises procedures, in the light of work preparation and supervisory activities. It implies mainly occupational skills and knowledge.

Level 4, 'specialist or middle manager', is responsible for his/her own work and has to account for his/her actions to his/her colleagues (non-hierarchical). In addition he bears explicit hierarchical responsibility; this responsibility concerns planning and/or administration and/or management and/or development of the whole production cycle. Furthermore he combines or devises new procedures. It implies specialist skills and knowledge and/or occupation-independent skills and knowledge.

At level 5, an occupational practitioner (professional) is responsible for his own work and has to account for his own actions (to colleagues, non-hierarchical). Work can involve both applying and combining/devising complex standard procedures and applying, combining/devising standard procedures for a broad range of activities. In addition, an occupational practitioner bears explicit hierarchical responsibility. This does not involve responsibility in an executive sense (i.e. monitoring and supervision), but rather responsibility in a formal, organisational sense. It implies specialised, occupation-independent skills and knowledge. A professional devises new procedures, tactical and strategic actions and has comprehensive skills with regard to policy development and execution.

These concepts are worked out in detail in order to place sectoral qualifications at a particular level. In addition, this format sets requirements related to the length of training for a specific qualification level and the entry conditions for the corresponding vocational education programmes. The latter criteria have less to do with the character of the vocational practice and more to do with the subsidy conditions of the Netherlands Ministry of Education.

The level of responsibility refers to the impact of activities on the occupational actions of others:

(a) the individual is responsible for his/her own activities only;

(b) non-hierarchical responsibility; meaning mutual responsibility for one's own activities and the activities of colleagues (in a team, group, gang);

(c) hierarchical responsibility in relation to monitoring, supervisory and managerial tasks.

The level of complexity indicates to what extent actions are based on standardised procedures:

(a) automated routines, mostly algorithms automatically executed;

(b) application of standard procedures, mostly non-automatic algorithms;

(c) combining standard procedures, mostly skills in problem-solving using familiar procedures;

(d) developing new procedures, application of problem-solving skills resulting in new solutions, possibly adding new aspects to an occupation.

The level of transfer indicates whether occupational skills can be applied in a variety of job positions:

(a) job-related skills, linked to a part of a production cycle;

(b) occupation-related skills, linked to production techniques;

(c) occupation-independent skills, applicable in a variety of occupations/jobs.

The length of training covers the minimum and maximum length of the course of a study programme at a specific qualification level:

(a) study programmes at level 1 must have a minimum of a half year and a maximum of one year;

(b) study programmes at level 2 must have a minimum of two and a maximum of three years;

(c) study programmes at level 3 must have a minimum of two and a maximum of four years;

(d) study programmes at level 4 must have a minimum of three and a maximum of four years.

Entry conditions vary. Vocational education programmes preparing for a level 1 or level 2 qualification are open to everyone; there are no preliminary education conditions. Vocational education programmes preparing for a level 3 or level 4 qualification are open to everyone either having a diploma of a lower type of general secondary education or having completed three years, a higher type of general secondary education or a level 2 qualification.

The Dutch descriptors of levels are as problematic as the English ones. In 1997, secondary vocational education curricula were adapted to this new qualification and level concept. This was an interesting test case for the application of the newly introduced criteria. The results were rather disappointing as the *ACOA* ([29]) concluded that *LOBs* ([30]) interpreted standards, qualifications and levels differently. As a result, certain sets of sector-based standards are identical to the traditional knowledge-based training goals that they were supposed to replace. Qualifications were supposed to be different with regard to organisation in units (formerly units were purely based on educational structures (subjects)) and the selection and wording of standards, which used to be knowledge (subject) based.

The *ACOA* committee also concluded that most *LOBs* adopted fairly formal arguments for allocating qualifications to levels. In fact, their arguments were almost identical to/copied from the definitions presented to them. Comparing the levels in the traditional educational structure and the levels in the new qualification structure shows practically no differences. The old primary, secondary and tertiary apprenticeship training programmes were allocated to qualification levels 2, 3 and 4 respectively. The tertiary apprenticeship programmes were classified as specialist training (level 4). Almost all traditional four-year *middelbaar beroepsonderwijs* courses (secondary vocational education ([31])) are allocated to level 4.

The rules of the game in allocating qualifications to levels do not appear to be clear. Using three different criteria (responsibility, complexity and transfer) generates confusion. Which of these criteria is the most important one? And if more than one degree of complexity, for example, can be identified in an occupation, which one should be selected? There is much confusion when several degrees of complexity, responsibility or transfer are identified in an occupation. In such a case, committees complain that the corresponding qualification 'cannot be allocated to a level properly'. There are terminology problems as well. Those intended to use the criteria are not familiar with terms like

---

([29]) The Independent Vocational Education and Labour Market Advisory Committee (*Advies Commissie Onderwijs Arbeidsmarkt*) commissioned by the Ministry of Education for the quality assessment of sector-related qualifications on all four levels.

([30]) *Landelijke organen beroepsonderwijs (LOBs)* are sector-based national training bodies responsible for the production of sector-specific qualifications. The task of the *LOBs* is aimed at the development of qualifications and standards for the four-level secondary vocational education system.

([31]) The term *middelbaar beroepsonderwijs (MBO)* (literally, secondary vocational education) might arouse some confusion as the meaning has changed. Before the new Act on VET and Adult Education was implemented in 1997, the term referred to four-year school-based vocational courses only. The new act labels all school-based and dual programmes, on level 1, 2, 3 or 4, as *middelbaar beroepsonderwijs*.

'automated routines' or 'standard procedures'. In addition, they associate complexity with the complexity and variety of working conditions and less with routines and procedures, i.e. the nature of work on a more abstract level.

5.5. United Kingdom (England and Wales)

The picture regarding levels in the English system is quite complex. The national framework of qualifications is intended to apply to all approved qualifications. It has five levels and three categories of qualification. This framework does not have descriptors attached to the levels, although for working purposes some have labels – for example, qualifications in the first three levels have the labels 'foundation', 'intermediate' and 'advanced' respectively. The levels are defined implicitly – that is, recognised qualifications are placed in the hierarchy of levels. The level thus gains meaning from the qualifications which have been placed at that level and their relationship with the qualifications placed in the adjacent higher and lower levels. The NVQ framework of levels applies to NVQs, which is one class of qualifications that fits into the third category –occupational qualifications– in the national framework. The levels for these qualifications have descriptors.

Figure 2. **The English national qualification framework**

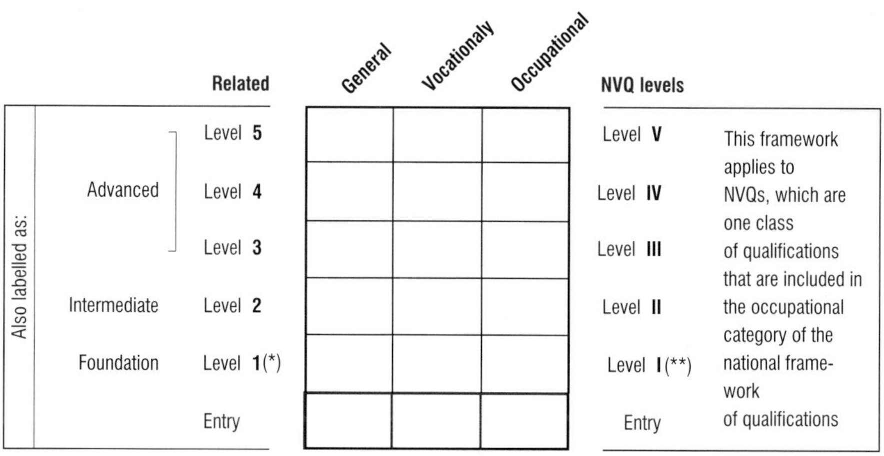

(*) Note that this level does not have descriptors.
(**) Note that this level does have descriptors.

The basic idea of the English NVQs is that they are output based. Standards indicate the functions that a person can perform, regardless of where and/or how the appropriate skills and knowledge were acquired. The same approach is used in the definition of the levels in the NVQ classification system. Levels express the difference between 'occupational competence' in terms of tasks to be performed, difficulty and complexity of the work. Crucially, the five-level framework typically seeks to describe characteristics of the work activity rather than the qualities and characteristics of the people operating at a given level.

The five NVQ levels are defined as follows:

(a) level I, occupational competence in performing a range of tasks under supervision;

(b) level II, occupational competence in performing a wider, more demanding range of tasks with limited supervision;

(c) level III, occupational competence required for satisfactory, responsible performance in a defined occupation or range of jobs;

(d) level IV, competence to design and specify defined tasks, products or processes and to accept responsibility for the work of others;

(e) level V, should reflect competence at professional level with mastery of a range of relevant knowledge and the ability to apply it at a higher level than IV.

This qualification levels framework contains internal tensions and problems. Not least of these is the problem of 'multidimensional tensions'. Statements at the different levels emphasise different aspects of performance, using them in complex mixes to derive the levels: supervision, responsibility; design (of tasks, products, etc.) and demand. With these criteria, the relative difficulty and complexity of qualifications appear to be clearly indicated. However, the criteria are sufficiently ambiguous to allow substantial variations across different occupational areas, depending on how they are interpreted by the relevant national organisations setting the standards and developing the qualifications. The commitment to defining the standards in terms of levels of performance, rather than the skills and knowledge required to operate at a given level, contributes to the lack of precision in the descriptors.

The level descriptors contain significant inconsistencies and problems. For instance, supervision as a defining concept (under supervision' or 'with limited supervision') appears in levels I and II, but not in levels III to V. It is essential to remember that the definition of 'level' focused on 'difficulty' and 'complexity' (of a course or award). 'Supervision' is not related to this in a clear way. It is highly contingent on the context in which a worker is operating – the specific work system, technology, importance and safety of the work, etc.

As a function of context, it does not necessarily relate to the skill level or capacity of an individual worker. There are also counter-examples, where simple tasks may require very low levels of supervision, if any. In contrast, some high-level professional work includes routine liaison and guidance by superiors of the overall direction of work, which is built in through high levels of strategic discussion, consultation and exchange. As with lower levels in the framework, such supervision is highly contingent on company-specific work systems.

Level IV states 'accept responsibility for the work of others'. The management function can be used to discriminate different types of job function but this is contingent on the work organisation and has a significant number of counter-examples. Newer work systems emphasise individuals at all levels of a work system taking greater responsibility for the quality and rate of work; many new jobs in the area of information and communication technology comprise individuals working discretely at a high level (in terms of intellectual demand, pressure, technical complexity, etc.). They no longer have to climb a traditional hierarchical or corporate ladder where each rank includes greater responsibility for the work of others or has greater complexity in the mix of work.

Design (of tasks, products, processes) is a key component of level IV and is particularly problematic. Job and task design can refer to a very specific technical job, undertaken by specialists. The emphasis on tasks, products and processes, whilst attempting to be comprehensive, actually mixes quite different roles. Product design is a very specific, technical function, which does not necessarily involve any extended management function. 'Design of tasks' contrasts with the way in which contemporary management roles tend to focus on monitoring and ensuring attainment of broad objectives rather than exercising control through the design of individual tasks. Whilst management functions can be concerned with the monitoring of tasks, products and processes, the design and specification of these are not a necessary part of such functions.

Hierarchies based on difficulty or demand are notoriously problematic. Work on hierarchies in mathematics suggests that many of the assumptions about hierarchies of difficulty derive from established patterns of instruction rather than intrinsic qualities of the content or operations. Demand and difficulty are also strongly related to individuals – what is difficult for one person is not necessarily difficult for another. It is a function of the relationship between the abilities, skills, knowledge and attitudes of an individual and the task/activity, rather than an intrinsic quality of the task/activity itself.

Complexity is an additional construct, which can be associated with demand. This holds more promise as a construct for differentiating levels of performance. The cognitive acceleration in science education project ([32]) has high-lighted the handling of multivariate problems as a feature of higher-order performance. Alongside this, complexity of job role as a function of being able to handle a range of tasks – rather than the complexity of individual tasks – is a key feature of the job competence model ([33]).

The NVQ descriptors thus remain problematic. In practice, in approving and developing qualifications, more attention is applied to the coherence of the hierarchy in an occupational area rather than whether individual qualifications conform exactly to the level descriptors. This is consistent with the move in the national qualifications framework towards an overall levels framework that has no descriptors and is intended to be highly inclusive (of different qualifications developed by different bodies for different purposes).

5.6. Summary

The identification of the number of levels is rather complex. Tertiary education might hide levels which are not yet formally identified in national qualification frameworks. Apart from this, there is the difference between the number of levels as they are formally identified within a system or education subsystem and the implicit number of levels throughout the national vocational qualifica-tion (or education) framework. The figures in this section represent the formalised levels throughout the various vocation (education) subsystems presented in this report. The number of levels varies from three (Spain) and (Germany), via five (England/NVQs and the Netherlands) to six (France).

Levels are defined differently. The criteria used to identify levels can be divided into six groups:

1. input criteria or admission requirements for education and training programmes delivering qualifications or for the assessment of qualifi-cations – for instance, the duration and type of occupational experience or preliminary education or training;
2. characteristics of the programmes delivering qualifications – for instance, the programmes' duration or the learning venues;
3. output criteria in terms of learning outputs – the attainment goals;
4. output criteria in terms of occupational practice or characteristics of work;

([32]) Adey, P. and Yates, C., *Better learning – A report from the cognitive acceleration in science educa-tion project,* Kings College, London, 1990.
([33]) Mansfield, R. and Mathews, D., *Job competence,* Further Education Staff College, 1985.

5. the position of a qualification in occupational hierarchies;
6. equation statements, formally stating the equality of qualifications at a certain level.

With the NVQs, England and Wales have a pure set of criteria as this framework only uses output criteria in terms of the characteristics of work (group 4), while the Dearing framework is an equating system in its purest form (group 6). France also has a pure set of criteria. Originally, the French classification system was created as a part of French economic planning policy and focused on prospective professional recruitment needs. Nowadays, the criteria are used to define the level of diplomas and to determine the 'value' of the study programmes and diplomas that do not belong to the initial vocational education system. The principles behind this French classification of levels are not concerned with the conditions of training but with the use that can be made of the levels of training in occupational practice. For this reason, French level criteria can be labelled as group 5 criteria, indicating how diplomas are linked to occupational positions.

In all the other countries, a mixed set of qualifications is applied. For example, German subsystem levels are defined by criteria taken from groups 1 (*Weiterbildungsberufe*), 2 and 4. Descriptors taken from groups 2, 3 and 4 are used in Spain. For application in VET, the Dutch four-level framework uses criteria taken from groups 1, 2 and 5 [34].

Referring to this classification of level criteria, the 1985 European five-level structure (see Annex 2) uses criteria taken from groups 2, 3, 4 and 5 in a somewhat inconsistent way. Criteria taken from group 2 ('training that gives entry to this level') and from group 5 ('this activity consists largely of practical work, which can be carried out independently') can be found in the definition of all levels. Criteria from group 3 can be found in the definition of level 3 only ('this implies more theoretical knowledge...'), while criteria taken from group 4 can be found in the definition of levels 4 and 5 ('...has a thorough command of the scientific background of the occupation').

Basically, the ISCED-97 classification of education levels (see Annex 3) is unidimensional as the content of educational activities is the key to the level concept. Its overall level concept is defined in terms of the content of the underlying educational activities, operationalised on the basis of multiple auxiliary criteria as proxies for the content (typical starting ages, length of the programme, entrance qualifications and entrance requirements, type of certification, etc.).

---

[34] In practice, Dutch qualifications are almost exclusively used to certify VET programmes and not for the assessment of prior learning. Dutch qualifications are, in fact, only obtainable via an educational pathway.

A fundamental aspect of these criteria is that they complement, rather than exclude, each other. By definition, ISCED also covers vocational and professional education and for these types of education the subject content and not the intended occupation was chosen as a classification criterion (³⁵).

The fact is that the quality of the criteria used to identify levels, whether a mixed set or a pure set, is not sufficient to guarantee an unproblematic use of qualification levels. This can be learnt from the use of the criteria in England and the Netherlands. In both countries, the level criteria should enable sector committees (national training organisations (NTOs), and *landelijke organen beroepsonderwijs (LOBs),* respectively) to position sector-based qualifications in the classification structure in respect of the characteristics of the occupations for which they are preparing. In essence, they should be able to provide a level designation for the respective qualifications.

However, in both countries the ambiguity of the definition of levels causes NTOs and *LOBs* to focus on relative level differences between the qualifications of their own sector (³⁶). The position proposed for a qualification in the national frameworks can often be better determined by its position relative to other qualifications and patterns of progression in the specific occupational sector, rather than by exact correspondence with level descriptors. Thus, the level assigned to a qualification strongly relates to the content of other qualifications in the framework. Industry bodies do not consider the precise equivalence of qualifications (in terms of technical content, intellectual demand, etc.) at the same level but in different occupational sectors to be such a crucial issue as a 'correct' hierarchy in the specific sector for which they are responsible. As a result, this approach to assigning levels to qualifications makes sense in the context of each specific sector, but results in poor connections with level definitions and equivalences across different sectors and in respect of interprofessional relationships.

Since levels convey status – reflected in the level hierarchy – the allocation of qualifications to levels can become the subject of powerful political and cultural pressure. In general, standard setting and classification have a very important social dimension as can be seen in examples taken from France, England and the Netherlands. In 1998–99, the French metallurgy sector requested a procedure of *homologation* for some of its *certificats de qualifications professionelles (CQP)* (³⁷). The sector took the step towards 'equivalence

---

(³⁵) *Fields of training (manual),* Cedefop and Eurostat, Thessaloniki and Luxembourg, 1999, note 1.

(³⁶) Sector-based classifications of qualifications tend to be ordinal scaled, rather than rational. The criteria are used to place qualifications on an ordinal scale, with reference to sector-based qualifications on the same or on other levels.

(³⁷) *Certificats de qualifications professionnelles* (Vocational qualification certificates).

through levels' even though it does not need this for its own human resources management purposes. The social partners of the individual sectors give a high level of legitimacy to these CQP from their position as generator and valuator of qualifications. To extend this legitimacy to training for other sectors, the choice was made to go through the *homologation* procedure. In England, attempts have been made to place qualifications on a higher level because these qualifications would then enjoy increased status [38]. Another example comes from the Netherlands. The Cedefop study, *The impact on vocational training of studies analysing and forecasting trends in occupations*, presents the case of a qualification that was allocated to a lower level than the most suitable one in terms of work content, because of the implications a higher level would have had on the salary scale [39].

---

[38] Oates, T., *An analysis of the implementation of levels frameworks in the English education and training system 1986 to 1999*, Qualifications and Curriculum Authority, 2000.

[39] DTI, *The impact on vocational training of studies analysing and forecasting trends in occupations*, Cedefop document, 1998.

6. The development and maintenance of standards and qualifications

Procedures used for the development and maintenance of standards and qualifications have the effect of making clear who actually decides on the content and composition of the competences of (future) professionals. What is the influence of industry, education and government? Should (frequently updated) standards reflect rapid developments in occupations or should they offer a durable basis, allowing a professional to play a part in these developments? Do the standards match the actual situation in professional practice or do they express the social consensus on what (future) professionals should know and be able to perform? Are standards the property of the companies and organisations where the occupations and tasks are performed or should the standards do justice to the opinions, values and interests of a number of parties? A lot of these questions can be answered by looking carefully at the relevant procedures [40].

A further issue is the relationship between the development of standards and the assessment of the quality of the standards. Should all standards meet specific criteria? If so, how stringent are these criteria and who is responsible for their verification? Procedures for updating standards and qualifications are described in this section. In all procedures, we encounter three elements, though the procedures differ in the relative weight given to each of these elements:
(a) a framework indicating the criteria which standards and qualifications must satisfy;
(b) procedures assessing whether standards and qualifications should be renewed, what the specifications for the new standards and qualifications will be and whether the newly produced standards and qualifications meet the criteria;
(c) methods for the development of standards and qualifications.

---

[40] See Cedefop (Sellin, B., 2000): *Anticipation of trends in occupations and qualifications*, published in www.trainingvillage.gr as a PDF file.

6.1. Germany

German qualifications are part of distinct subsystems in vocational education and different approaches are taken to keep standards up to date. The approaches relate mainly to the study programme plans (*Lehr-, Studien-* or *Ausbildungspläne* or *-ordnungen*) or examination regulations (*Prüfungsordnungen*) with the differences evident in the number and type of organisations that are involved in the development process. Decision-making about placing qualifications or standards at a particular level is limited to *Ausbildungsberufe* and *Weiterbildungsberufe*. The government at national or federal level lays down a framework for curricula in the *Ausbildungsordnungen, Fortbildungsordnungen* and framework curricula (*Rahmenvereinbarungen* for *Lehr-* and *Ausbildungspläne*).

Training regulations for the *Ausbildungsberufe* arise from a lengthy negotiation process involving a large number of organisations (employers' and employees' organisations, representatives of the federal government and federal states, the Ministries of Education and Research, and Economic Affairs, and/or specific ministries such as agriculture, health, etc., depending on the sector). Reaching a consensus in situations where interests may be in conflict is often a lengthy process. However, this consensus is important as the qualifications in the most important subsystem, the *Ausbildungsberufe*-based *Ausbildungsordnungen*, have legal status. Social rights, level of payment and career possibilities depend on the possession of a particular *Ausbildungsberuf* qualification. In addition, the commitment of business and industry is necessary for the assessment of relevance of a *Beruf* and the organisation of company-based training for this *Beruf*. An apprentice has the right to sue his/her employer when the company does not organise training opportunities inside or outside the company for all parts of the *Ausbildungsberuf*.

To ensure commitment, a two-stage approach to the framework produces a new regulation before the contents of the study programmes are developed:

(a) a research and development stage during which the Federal Institute for Vocational Training (*BIBB*) draws up documents for decision-making on matters relating to the structure and content of an envisaged training regulation;

(b) a preliminary stage during which employers' federations, trade unions, the federal government and the *Länder* governments reach agreement on implementing the training regulation project and determine the key parameters. These key parameters and the project concept are documented in a project application dossier prepared by the competent sector minister with *BIBBs* support.

The development of training regulations of the *Schulberufe* and the study programme for *Weiterbildungsberufe* supervised by the federal states is less complicated. They are developed by schools and representatives from the respective federal state ministry of education. The same method is used at the tertiary level where the development of standards and of new educational programmes, as well as the updating of existing curricula and degrees, is largely up to the universities themselves. The federal states exercise a controlling function, whether these are in accordance with the framework law and the specific laws for higher education (see Section 4). The State mainly provides formal frameworks, with the exception of those areas of study which finish with a State examination, i.e. in medicine and law as well as in teacher education.

The more vocationally or professionally oriented the course, the more representatives from the relevant field are involved in the initiation and development of, or changes to, the programme and qualification. This is the case at the tertiary level, above all for the *Fachhochschulen* and the *Berufs-akademien* ([41]). In the development process of the federal *Weiterbildungs-berufe,* the initiative lies with the social partners. After having reached internal agreement, the parties with an interest in having an advanced qualification established, acting via the apex organisations of the two sides of industry, submit a corresponding application to the Federal Ministry of Education and Research which, acting as lead agency, contacts the other federal ministries concerned. The Federal Minister for Education and Research examines the need for regulatory action on the basis of hearings (ministries, social partners, applicants, parties concerned) and takes a decision on the political framework and subsequent procedures.

As a matter of principle, it is always the body issuing the regulation that is responsible for keeping the qualification up to date. As far as the federally regulated initial and advanced qualifications are concerned, the social partners have considerable influence in determining when a qualification should be updated or new ones introduced. Only if they arrived at a basic consensus and agree so-called corner data *(Eckdaten)* do the federal institute and the respective ministries of the federal government become active. They do not, in principle, take the initiative on their own, even if they may push the social partners forward. How they carry out the corresponding exchange of experience and views is a matter left to the social partners themselves.

In the case of full-time school-based qualifications, the initiative lies with the federal states which regulate them, though they may be pushed by other

---

([41]) These professional institutes for higher adult education exist only in a few federal states; the titles delivered are called *Diplom* (BA).

local and regional authorities, colleges or socioeconomic groups related to the respective occupational field. Experts consider that intervals of five years are appropriate for checking whether the minimum standards laid down are still in line with the demands of technological, organisational, economic and social change.

As far as initial vocational qualifications are concerned, the federal government and the social partners agreed in 1995 that development procedures should be accelerated. An important issue here is reaching agreement on the extent of the reforms needed: whether it is just the content and possibly also the examination requirements which should be adapted to meet changing needs or whether there is a need for a fundamental review and redrafting of the underlying concept. Once the social partners agree, the ministry has to decide on applications for updating within a period of three months. If it is only the content and the examination requirements that are to be modified, the updating process should take no longer than one year to be completed. In the case of a fundamental structural redrafting, a period of two years before formal approval is usual.

Taking note of the rapidity of developments in professional practice, it is no longer sufficient to take action when it is clear that standards need to be revised, with the inevitable loss of time associated with this procedure. Therefore, in 1998, on the initiative of the national Ministry of Education and Research (*Bundesministerium für Bildung und Forschung*) an early warning system (*Früherkennungssystem*) for the development of qualifications was launched. Early recognition of developments, for example through a monitoring system, should enable rapid response to developments.

6.2. Spain

The General Council for Vocational Training (*Consejo General de la Formación Profesional, CGFP*) is responsible for controlling, maintaining and updating vocational standards used in the education system. The *CGFP* was established in 1997 as 'a tripartite consultative body involving management and union organisations and public administration organisations and, furthermore, as an advisory body to the government (*MEC*) in matters of vocational training' [42]. The national government, the autonomous regions and the social partners are represented in the *CGFP*. The main competences of the *CGFP* are:

---

[42] *Real Decreto* 1684/1997 of 7 November 1997.

(a) to evaluate and control the implementation of the national programme and propose its updating, without detriment to the autonomous regions' powers in this area;

(b) to report on the planned syllabuses and qualifications corresponding to the various vocational training degrees and specialities, and the professional certificates in matters of occupational vocational training and, where appropriate, their academic or professional *homologation* with the corresponding levels of regulated vocational training, without threatening the competences of the State Schools Council in these matters.

In the field of initial vocational education, the drawing-up of the *Catalogue of FPR qualifications* [43] is a major attempt both to update the syllabus and to streamline the training supply and try to relate it to the evolution of jobs and the qualification needs of the productive system. With the experts from the *MEC*, education/training experts (professors, teachers and trainers from the different segments of vocational training) and labour experts (professional engineers, technicians, and/or managers of companies, employer and union organisations from every sector) are involved in designing and drawing up qualifications.

The syllabus of regulated vocational training (*Catalogue of FPR qualifications)* is regularly updated using sector studies. The studies provide information on business structures, the evolution of business activities and their effect on the design of occupations, vocational training needs, and the content and occupational itineraries of the various sectors and subsectors of the Spanish economy.

Representatives of the public administration/ministries, sector experts, union representatives and management representatives of the companies create a sector working group that elaborates the sector, studies and defines the professional profiles from each one of these sectors (see Figure 3). From this definition of professional profiles, both vocational systems (regulated and occupational) define the educational curricula leading to a qualification.

---

[43] *FPR* stands for *formación profesional reglada* (regulated vocational education).

Figure 3. **Parties involved in the production of sector studies in Spain**

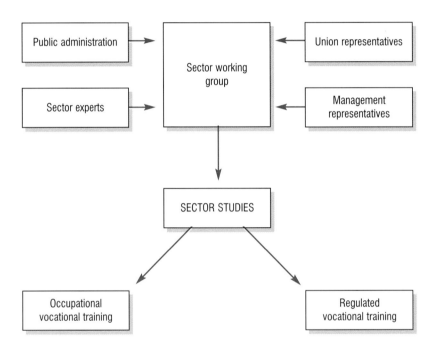

The procedure for drawing up the *CTP*([44]) has involved a broad and unprecedented process of study and analysis of the production system alongside the participation and advice of management and union representatives, specialists from companies, technicians, etc.

The methodology used to draw up professional qualifications is mainly qualitative, involving functional analysis of tasks and competences of the 'professional families' produced in the sector studies conducted by *INEM*. The forecasts for new qualifications in the professional families, training needs and the emergence of new occupations anticipate the medium term. Producing the *CTP* has constituted important progress in the analysis and updating of the qualifications in Spain. At this moment, the *CTP* consists of professional profiles for 24 professional families; another two have yet to be developed.

([44]) *CTP* stands for *Catálogo de Títulos Profesionales,* the catalogue of all titles in regulated vocational education.

The profiles were developed in four phases, carried out mainly by the Vocational Training Committee, beginning with analysis of the economic, technological, organisational, occupational and training aspects of the sectors. These analyses include the sector studies conducted by the Spanish Office of Employment in collaboration with the Ministry of Education and Culture.

Based on the conclusions of the sector study, a functional analysis of the production processes was carried out by a work group consisting of technological experts from the sector and education experts, including from governmental bodies responsible for the sector's professional or labour regulations. The experts identified the functions that people must be able to perform in order to achieve the performance asked for by productive organisations. These functions are formulated as skill titles and are grouped together accordingly to constitute the professional profiles of the qualifications.

In the third phase, taking the professional profiles as a reference, the basic knowledge, abilities, skills and attitudes necessary to obtain the professional skill defined by the profile were identified. This construct was expressed in close connection with the corresponding achievement goals and evaluation criteria. Similarly, the content of each training programme was determined to enable pupils to obtain the aforementioned competences.

In the fourth phase, the qualifications and certificates were compared, with the participation of management, union and professional organisations and other government bodies.

Since the economic and social agreement (*Accuerdo Económico y Social, AES*) in 1985, the intervention of the *CGFP* to arrange and supervise the process has been ensured.

6.3. France

The Ministry of Education compiles French national diplomas. The ministry is advised in this matter by 19 sector occupational/professional advisory committees (*commissions professionnelles consultatives, CPC*). Representatives of various ministries, specialists, representatives of parents and social partners, representatives of the respective sector and professional grouping form the *CPC*. The *CPC* advise about the adjustment of the diplomas that are related to their sector. They ensure the quality of the occupational activity frames of references. *CPC* activities cover professional education and training at various levels. Any member of a *CPC* can forward a request for updating, reviewing or creating a new diploma.

The procedure for the development or adjustment of diplomas consists of two main steps. In the first, the need to adjust a diploma is studied in response to a request either from the ministry itself or from industry. If the advice from the ministry and the relevant *CPC* is positive, the second phase is undertaken. Under the supervision of the *CPC,* two individual work groups develop, in succession, a profile and a new certification frame of reference. The first work group has experts from professional practice. In the second, teachers and educational inspectors are consulted.

The reference documents developed in this procedure are used for examination purposes. Biases in the use of the reference documents are fought against through a high standardisation of the evaluation process, i.e. the examination process. National and regional inspectors play an important role in this context, as do national centralised examination procedures.

In general, each diploma is reviewed approximately every five years. A national classification (a list) of training specialities exists (*nomenclature de formation*) as well as a national classification (a list) of occupations (*nomenclature de professions*) called *PCS (professions catégories socio-professionnelles)*. Both have statistical purposes, but key players in the labour market and in the training field use them extensively. In *PCS,* there is a qualitative element in that it also reflects the socioeconomic category of the occupation including its position in the hierarchy of occupations.

6.4. The Netherlands

A total of 22 national organisations develop the standards for vocational education on secondary level (*landelijke organen voor het beroepsonderwijs, LOBs*). An *LOB* is expected to monitor developments in its sector, keeping the qualifications and standards up to date. It manages the composition and content of the qualifications of the sector.

The initiative for the development or adjustment of a qualification rests with the *LOB*. The Ministry of Education, Culture and Science does not have to be consulted about this. The *LOB*, where the sector-specific social partners take the lead themselves, is free to decide the kind and volume of adjustments. It can limit this to updating just some of the elements of one single qualification, but can also restructure a number of qualifications of differing levels at the same time.

The actual development process of standards and qualifications consists of two steps. In the first step, the professional profiles are developed. Dependent upon the extent of the adjustment, one or more professional profiles are developed. The *LOB* is free to decide which investigative methods it will use to achieve a new or renewed professional profile. Empirical surveys as well as (video) conferences of expert meetings are applied. Finally, the investigation must lead to the laying-down of one or more professional profiles by the sector's social partners.

In the second phase, sector-based social partners develop one or more vocational education profiles in cooperation with representatives from the schools (a *LOB* in fact). The result, called a *beroepsonderwijsprofiel* (vocational education profile), is the Dutch equivalent of what in this report is defined as a qualification.

The difference between professional profiles and vocational education profiles is crucial. A professional profile is drawn up by social partners and reflects the current situation in a profession. Social partners and the education field draw up a vocational education profile (qualification) together. It can be composed from several professional profiles. In other words, the breadth of a qualification is set down in consultation between industry and education. In a vocational education profile, the standards, divided into units, are included. They are formally approved and published by the Ministry of Education, Culture and Science after consultation of the *ACOA*. Only education programmes preparing for these ministerial-approved qualifications are considered for government subsidy.

A characteristic of this procedure is that the state has set out a general framework within which the parties involved are required to operate. The Ministry of Education, Culture and Science keeps its distance, attributing to the *ACOA* the role of developing new proposals for criteria with which qualifications and standards must comply. Only in this indirect way does the government have an influence on the quality and composition of standards and qualifications.

In higher professional education, qualifications are developed in a more informal way. Invited by the schools, a group of professionals produces a profile for the respective profession. Schools cooperate in developing a so-called educational profile covering about 4 720 out of the 6 720 study hours a course in higher professional education will comprise. The key concept is self-regulation, with a high degree of autonomy in the light of professional, sectoral and regional needs and trends.

6.5. United Kingdom (England and Wales)

If an organisation wishes a qualification to be approved as part of the national framework of qualifications, the stages of development of national standards are regulated, with a routine pattern applied across all occupational sectors and levels. In the occupational segment of the system, national qualifications are developed by designated national training organisations (NTOs). These often commission experts or consultants experienced in standards development.

With the focus on occupational standards, the national standards have an industry-wide orientation, but are developed through analysis of individual enterprises' work organisation and internal company-specific standards. The principal requirement is that the standards should relate to competence rather than simply express the requirements of training or vocational education programmes.

Draft standards are required to go through wide consultation with enterprises, for validity and transparency. These form the basis of qualifications, which are developed in conjunction with national awarding bodies, which are then submitted to the QCA for admission to the national framework. More than one awarding body may develop qualifications relating to the same set of occupational standards. The QCA will use the separate criteria that have been laid down for specific types of qualifications, for example for GCSEs (general certificates of secondary education), for NVQs, etc. Management of the system of organisations developing the occupational standards which form the basis of NVQs and other key qualifications admitted to the occupational segment of the system previously was the responsibility of the DfEE (Department for Education and Employment) but passed in 1997 to the QCA.

An NVQ must be based on the national standards; this is now more important than whether the qualification follows the exact form of the units developed at the outset of the implementation of the NVQ system. However, qualifications must be expressed in the form of units, and must be available on a national basis. As part of the submission and approval process, the QCA checks whether quality assurance and administration systems for the qualification meet the criteria laid down, including those relating to equal opportunities.

More than one awarding body may work with an NTO in order to deliver the same, or broadly similar, NVQs. Similarly, an NTO may work with more than one awarding body to develop complementary qualifications or qualifications in different areas and/or levels of the national framework. A few NTOs are also awarding bodies themselves, although this is a situation which the QCA and DfEE do not encourage, due to potential problems of conflict of interests, or monopolistic tendencies.

In the procedure for developing new standards, an NTO takes the initiative, commissions research (occupational analysis) and develops (draft) standards. The QCA has a supervising and approving role. The allocation of qualifications to levels is proposed by the submitting awarding body. It proposes to the QCA the level in the national framework to which a specific qualification relates and provides justification. The QCA checks the submission and negotiates with the awarding body and the NTO if the justification is not adequate. Table 3 indicates the timescale for each of the stages in the NVQ development process.

Table 4. **Timescales and stages in the NVQ development process**

TIMESCALES (*)	STAGES IN THE DEVELOPMENT PROCESS
Stages 1 and 2 (approximately six months)	**Stage 1** NTO approaches QCA with proposal to develop national standards in a specific occupational area
	Stage 2 QCA judges merit of proposal in conjunction with SQA (Scottish Qualifications Authority) and consults with Welsh and Northern Ireland bodies
stage 3 (between three and six months)	**Stage 3** After formal approval of proposal, NTO begins analysis of occupational area; this includes empirical analysis of content of work, plus consultation to verify content and language of standards
stages 4 and 5 (approximately three months)	**Stage 4** NTO submits draft standards to QCA, to original group which approved development work
	Stage 5 Potential refinement following recommendations of QCA approval group
stage 6 (approximately three months)	**Stage 6** After final approval and issuing of contract, national standards used for developing qualifications in conjunction with national awarding body

(*) The timescales vary from sector to sector and depend on whether or not significant problems are experienced in the development work.

For the development of national standards, the battery of analysis techniques for analysing occupational competence includes work process analysis, Delphi methods, critical incident analysis, analytical work deriving from socio-psychological study of work, task or functional analysis. Whatever the analysis approach used, the QCA must be confident that the NTO has undertaken adequate empirical analysis of the occupational functions described in the standards. It must also have undertaken adequate consultation with industry and other interests (trade unions, professional associations, etc.) to ensure that the standards represent the requirements of the occupational area.

Standards are currently approved for a maximum of five years. There is no formal minimum period, but the shortest period to date has been two years. The average duration of approval is three years.

6.6. Summary

It is interesting to see that the methods for analysing developments in sectors and occupations are quite similar. Empirical studies are used in all the countries, whether existing ones or studies specially commissioned for the purpose of the development of standards and qualifications. Furthermore, all the countries work with frameworks indicating the criteria that standards and qualifications which are to be developed have to satisfy.

Major differences can be found in the procedures assessing whether standards and qualifications should be renewed and whether the newly produced standards and qualifications meet the criteria. In England, France and the Netherlands, standing organisations or commissions are responsible for the maintenance of the standards and qualifications of a sector. For qualifications previously approved as a part of the national framework, English commissions are allowed to start an adjustment process only with the consent of the national agency, the QCA. The results of the development work must also be submitted to the QCA. This is partly the case for France but not for the Netherlands.

In the Netherlands central management is absent. Sector-based bodies *(LOBs)* have a large amount of freedom in the development and establishment of standards and qualifications. The role of the government is restricted due to the prior establishment of the criteria that all standards and qualifications must meet. In France, the *CPC* have a consultative voice and the government tends towards compromise. The final decision rests with the Ministry of Education and its *DESCO (Direction de l'Enseignement Scolaire*: Directorate for School Education).

In Germany, broadly composed committees are set up when a study programme (*Lehr-* or *Ausbildungsplan*) is to be renewed. The social partners and the government are represented in these committees. The social partners nominate experts doing the actual job and are strongly involved in the process in reviewing the work of the experts. Besides the study programme, plans must comply with the criteria laid down by the government. This procedure, however, concerns only the *Aus-* and *Fortbildungsberufe* and not the *Schulberufe,* most of the *Weiterbildungsberufe* and not at all the *Hochschulberufe.*

Spanish qualifications are the subject of tripartite control as a national council composed of government representatives, social partners and regions supervises the development of all qualifications.

7. The classification of qualifications at tertiary level

All over Europe, the number of people qualified at tertiary level is growing. OECD statistics for 1996 claim that in a number of countries more than 50 % of the relevant age group qualify at a national education system's tertiary level [45]. The growth of tertiary education is reflected in a growing variety of courses in terms of duration, qualification titles and organisations providing tertiary-level qualifications. The proliferation of tertiary education provisions is, in fact, inspired by the growing popularity of this type of education with students and in the labour market. This development towards *Teriärisierung der Berufs-ausbildung* (tertiarisation of VET), as this phenomenon is called in Germany, can be seen across Europe. With the introduction of new qualifications, tertiary education providers are responding to qualification demands in the labour market and a still increasing variety of students, particularly as institutes that traditionally provide tertiary education are autonomous in defining new qualifications and standards. In this process, it has become obvious that it is increasingly difficult to make an adequate distinction between the sub-degree levels at a tertiary level in some countries and the level 4 qualifications in other systems at the upper secondary level.

In this section, we will answer the question of how these developments are reflected in the number and definition of levels in national qualification frameworks. Are current qualification structures thought to be suitable for the absorption of this autonomous proliferation of tertiary-level qualifications? What are the national and international answers to this growing lack of transparency?

7.1. The position of tertiary qualifications in qualification frameworks

Vocational qualification systems such as the European five-level structure, the English NVQ framework and the Dutch five-level structure focus on secondary-level qualifications at four levels while tertiary-level qualifications are supposed

---

[45] OECD, *Education at a glance*, OECD indicators, Paris, 1998.

to be covered with one single level, namely level 5 ([46]). These three frameworks, in particular, have their roots in secondary vocational education. See, for example, Article 2 of the EEC Council decision on European qualification levels: 'The work referred to in paragraph 2 shall first and foremost concentrate on the occupational qualifications of skilled workers...' (Article 2, point 2).

In the Netherlands, the five-level structure was developed for secondary vocational education, covering only the first four levels of this framework. As stated in Section 3, tertiary vocational education, labelled as level 5, does not use this level definition as it feels itself as a part of the higher education infrastructure ([47]).

In England and Wales, in particular, level 5 NVQs are not widely used as universities and schools for higher professional education strongly prefer to develop their own study programmes instead of implementing NVQs. However, whereas in England a new concept has been launched for a qualification framework for tertiary vocational education, the Netherlands intends to implement the proposals formulated in the recent Bologna Declaration (1999).

Current discussions in Spain concentrate on the impact of the introduction of the European five-level structure. Not surprisingly, most attention is paid to the implications for secondary vocational education in terms of the definition of qualifications. So far, tertiary vocational education is only marginally affected by these debates. In Germany, the growing numbers of tertiary qualifications and their impact on level structures are not an issue for a national debate. Germany lacks a national qualification structure. Decisions on the definition of qualifications and the introduction of new qualifications are taking place within the traditional framework for higher education policy-making. The revisited German framework law on higher education (1998) allows the implementation of consecutive programme structures with the delivery of bachelor and masters degrees ([48]).

Qualification structures equally covering secondary vocational and tertiary professional qualifications can be found in France and in the English national qualification framework. Levels I, II and III of the French six level structure cover tertiary qualifications. These levels correspond to the three cycles in French tertiary education: level III refers to an initial two-year cycle, leading to a diploma from, for instance, *instituts universitaires de technologie (IUT)*. Level

---

([46]) In England, short tertiary programmes, provided by secondary vocational education or tertiary vocational education institutes, are also labelled as level 4.

([47]) See also Volume 3.

([48]) The German Science Council (*Wissenschaftsrat*) recently recommended replacing the traditional parallel structure by an internationally recognised three-evel structure: bachelor, master and doctorate (PhD) degrees. This is in line with the proposals in the Bologna Declaration.

II refers to diplomas to be obtained after a four-year (undergraduate) study programme and level I represents (postgraduate) doctorate degrees. This system of levels, introduced in 1969, is intended to classify all diplomas according to their respective objectives. New diplomas are classified into one of these levels, regardless of differences in programmes, or the quality and status of the institutes providing the courses. Thus, there seems to be another (rather hidden) structure within this three-level (meta-) framework.

A suggestion in the 1997 English Dearing report on higher education is interesting and relevant. The report suggests tackling this growing lack of transparency in the field of tertiary qualifications by implementing a qualification framework particularly covering tertiary qualifications [49]. This proposal is an example of the much wider trend towards developing a qualification framework for tertiary education independent of, or, in terms of definitions and criteria, only loosely related to, secondary education frameworks. The Lisbon (1997) Convention and Sorbonne (1998) and Bologna (1999) Declarations are also examples of this trend.

Basically, in the Bologna (1999) Declaration, 28 European countries agreed to introduce a coherent three-level framework for tertiary qualifications: a graduate (bachelor) level, to be obtained after three years of study; a postgraduate (master's) level to be obtained after five years; and a doctorate (PhD) level to be obtained after at least eight years of study. It is interesting to note that the development of a common structure for tertiary education is promoted within a European framework. It is also interesting to note that, even in the Dearing example, the duration of the education process has been taken into account in the definition of levels in addition to the outcomes. Far more than is the case with some of the qualification structures presented in the other sections of this report, these structures seem to be much more linked to an education system, which in this case is the tertiary education system.

---

[49] National Committee of Inquiry into Higher Education (CIHE), *Education in the learning society,* the Dearing report, HMSO, London, 1997. This framework is still under discussion. According to planning, it is foreseen that a definite concept will be delivered in 2000. The proposal suggests the introduction of eight levels, thus covering all qualifications of degrees and sub-degrees.

7.2. Summary

Tertiary education is faced with a rapid growth across Europe, both in terms of numbers of students as in the variety of courses and levels. Together with the growing significance of tertiary education for economic development and international labour market mobility, this development instigated a Europe-wide discussion on the need for greater international transparency and coherent classification. With the policy framework of the Lisbon Convention and the Sorbonne and Bologna Declarations, EU Member States are implementing a common European two-level (bachelor-master's) infrastructure for initial tertiary (professional) education. This framework should also be suitable for the assessment of prior learning. Apart from the Dearing proposal, this EU policy framework seems to be the focus point for national policy-making in European Member States with regard to the level structure of tertiary education.

Taking the recent proliferation of tertiary education into account, a European two- or three-level framework is surprisingly simple. Moreover, the duration and not the learning outcomes seem to be the most important criteria for demarcation. This will not be sufficient for international transparency and comparability. Traditionally, learning outcomes are defined by the tertiary education institutes themselves. Most tertiary education providers and universities define their own courses, linking institute-based certificates to their education programmes. As we see these institutes allowing their students to compose their own study programme (*Modularisierung von Studiengängen*), one wonders what these levels will actually say about somebody's qualification.

The Sorbonne and Bologna Declarations definitely resulted in international demand for more transparency at national and transnational level. They introduced the concept of a European classification system for tertiary qualifications. However, additional steps with regard to the compatibility and comparability of (outcome-based) standards and qualifications will be needed from the great variety of education providers in order to assess the actual equivalence of qualifications.

8. The European 1985 five-level classification framework and the national structures

The decision of the European Council on the comparability of vocational training qualifications among the Member States was passed in 1985. The five-level structure was introduced as an instrument to facilitate effective comparison between training offers in the Member States. In this section, we will analyse the relationship between the European 1985 five-level structure and national structures from two angles:

(a) whether or not the European system was a source of inspiration for the reforms in national qualification classification systems implemented after 1985;

(b) the similarities and differences between the descriptors and definitions used in the European five-level system and national classification systems.

This will allow assessment of the extent to which the European framework, and its application in the European comparability exercise ([50]), served as a source of inspiration for the countries adjusting classification frameworks around or after 1985, in particular England, the Netherlands and Spain.

8.1. Germany

The long-standing German vocational education system has always maintained a difficult relationship with the European five-level framework. The basis of the problems lies in the difference in the 'valuation' of learning venues other than schools. For the purposes of determining training levels, the five-level system links output criteria, for instance the ability to execute practical work

---

([50]) The European comparability exercise linked to the Council decision on comparability of qualifications from 1985 and put into practice by Cedefop on behalf of the European Commission between 1986 and 1993. A total of 19 occupational sectors and more than 200 occupational profiles were defined and national certificates were allocated to these common definitions until 1993 (see the respective European Official Journals, C series.

autonomously, with input criteria, i.e. the completion of specific initial courses such as a *Berufsausbildung* or a *Fachausbildung.*

In view of the fact that specific mention is made of apprenticeship being located at level 2 of the European framework, it can be concluded that the European classification was developed from a full-time education perspective. Consequently, those who graduated from apprenticeships were regarded as skilled workers (level 2) and not as 'technicians' trained in full-time schools as in France. This perspective evidently assumes that 'higher' (level 3) qualifications cannot be obtained via an apprenticeship that is mainly based on work experience and in-company training.

The Germans reproach the European system for not treating this distinction carefully; the learning venue (school, company) is not to be considered the same as learning content (theory, practice) [51]. With such an approach, the German dual system is placed structurally on a lower level (as regards content) than similar training systems in other Member States.

In fear of the consequences of a low position in the European five-level system, the *Institut der Deutschen Wirtschaft* (Institute of the German Economy, Cologne) commissioned a study on the effect of the European five-level system on the classification of German vocational qualifications (1995). The study aimed 'to explore the practical significance of the five-level system for the holders of vocational qualifications and for German companies' (Koch, 1995, p. 2). The first issue researched was the extent to which German companies were assuming a negative impact on their competitiveness in European markets as a result of the low classification of German qualifications by the five-level system (e.g. when bidding for orders).

In general terms, the study showed that the majority of the companies, associations and organisations were not familiar with the five-level system. The few which were familiar with it denied that it was having an impact on their competitiveness vis-à-vis their European rivals, at least at that time (1995). The study further found that German companies' competitiveness could be adversely affected in the future if proof of compliance with certain quality standards laid down by a contractor were to be judged on the basis of the five-level system.

---

[51] For the allocation of training offers to levels in the comparability exercise, the skilled workers' level definition was the deciding factor while learning venues were not taken into account. This less orthodox use of the criteria did not lead to a formal adaptation of the level definitions of the European 1985 framework.

8.2. Spain

The Spanish classification system for secondary vocational education has two levels. Following the 1990 educational reform, these levels are compatible with levels 2 and 3 of the European system. The explanation of this reform, 'this organisation is based on the structure of the training levels drawn up by the Commission of the European Communities', however, makes it clear that no new professional classification system was created. Rather, the categories from the European five-level structure were formally used for the allocation of Spanish levels that were not changed substantially. Spanish education standards and the European five-level structure are represented in Table 4.

Comparing the old education system (1970) and the current system (1990), an allocation problem is seen. In the old system, accepting the current divisions of levels established by the European Union, vocational qualifications corresponded to levels 1 and 2, whereas these qualifications in the new system now correspond to levels 2 and 3.

In 1988, the draft reform of technical/occupational education proposed a correlation between the qualifications and the five levels of professional proficiency mentioned above, which seemed congruent and significant. It was initially proposed that module 2 (current intermediate programme) should correspond with professional proficiency level 2 to skilled implementation, and module 3 (current advanced programme) should correspond with level 3, to technicians and middle managers, but this correlation was abandoned.

In the subsequent development of the reform concluded with the *LOGSE*, a terminology of qualifications was produced (technician for intermediate qualifications, and advanced technician for advanced qualifications), which led to confusion as it clashed with the customary meaning of these terms (the advanced technician was, and is, an engineer) thereby hampering transparency.

In the light of these differences, there is a risk of vocational training qualifications still being merely an academic reference, with very little influence on the actual labour market and, for the same reason, invalid in supporting an updated classification, as could and should be expected. They define the preparatory training that gives access to a level according to the nomenclature of the old education system. It is likely that there will be serious mismatches in the medium term between the classification systems of the education system and the labour market.

With the reform of the education system, and the reform of vocational training, professional profiles were constructed according to two factors: their suitability for the productive system and their comparability with the EU's levels 2 and 3.

Table 4. **Two Spanish education systems and the European five-level framework compared**

EDUCATION SYSTEM (1970)	CURRENT EDUCATION SYSTEM (1990)	AGE	EU LEVELS (1990)
Advanced technical college or university faculties (engineer or graduate)	Advanced technical college or university faculties (engineer or graduate)	22y +	5
University college (technical engineer or graduate)	University college (technical engineer or graduate)	20–21	4
	Advanced training programmes (advanced technician)	19	3
Second grade vocational training (expert technician)		18	
	University orientation course / Intermediate training programmes *(technician)* / *Bachillerato (Bachiller)*	17	2
		16	
First grade vocational training (assistant technician) / Unified and multipurpose baccalaureate	Compulsory secondary education (secondary education graduate)	15	
		14	
Basic general education *(EGB)* (school graduate or certificate on completion of *EGB* course)		13	1
	Primary education	6–12	
Pre-school education	Infant education	0–5	

8.3. France

The basic characteristics of the French framework were not altered after the introduction of the European classification framework. The question of whether the European model had an influence on the French system of levels must be answered negatively. In fact, the converse is true. The European five levels were, by and large, inspired by the French structure. The model is compatible with the French system although it is less detailed in its definitions. At the highest and lowest levels, France has more differentiated levels. Therefore, the French think European structures generate some distortion with regard to French practice. Compromises had to be made. The French set vocational and general academic achievement at upper secondary school level on an equal footing but only in formal terms. The social reality of it is different. Also, the first-level vocational diplomas (*CAP* and *BEP*) require less training years than the *baccalauréat* and they do not lead to the same level of jobs. However, it has been agreed to group them together at ISCED level 3 and, in that sense, it is felt that European systems 'mishandle' national systems. In a European dimension, the relevance of a supranational system cannot be ignored. It represents an important tool for comparisons, negotiations and understanding of local systems. The outcome of its establishment is, however, as much a matter of political negotiation as a matter of scientific argument.

The enquiries conducted for the French report showed that the European five-level system had no practical existence as such in France. The employment services in charge of managing the EURES system were contacted for comment. They replied that the European five-level system was never really used by French services for placement purposes and that it is regarded as obsolete ([52]).

8.4. The Netherlands

The current Dutch qualification framework for secondary vocational education was developed during 1992–93 and implemented in 1997. The commission that developed the framework took pains over the choice and definition of classification criteria. For this purpose, it studied the criteria and definitions from

---

([52]) The EURES network uses a formalised database of job offers that does not take account of training 'levels'. Two main elements are used that may be seen, in combination, as equivalent to the idea of levels: ISCO and NACE. These two international classifications have more or less been equated with similar French ones.

the English (NVQ), the Australian (ASF) and the European five-level systems. From the English system, it derived the principle that in the qualification structure no characteristics of study programmes should be described, but only skill and/or competence-based standards that could be acquired through quite different provision of education and training and/or experience.

Although the European framework was taken as a reference document, however, the content and characteristics of definitions retained do not really permit the establishment of a direct relationship between the European and the Dutch qualification framework. In the definitive proposal, the following reference is made: '... And as a result of being linked to the European SEDOC classification international mobility is stimulated. The diplomas are simpler to compare and easier to exchange...' [53]. Closer inspection reveals that this reference, in terms of level descriptors, is not substantial. In this perspective, it is amazing that in the Netherlands it is often claimed that the Dutch system was copied from the European five-level framework (see Table 5).

In the development process of the secondary vocational education four-level structure, the determination of the number of levels was not a point of discussion. A fourth level was added to the original three levels of secondary vocational education. This new level, the lowest in the classification, was added to include qualifications offering employment opportunities to people with no or discontinued preliminary training. It might be true that the idea of introducing a new semi-skilled qualification level (level 1) was inspired by the already existing European five-level structure. Research conducted for the Netherlands report produced no conclusive evidence for this statement, nor any to the contrary.

8.5. United Kingdom (England and Wales)

In 1986, the National Council for Vocational Qualifications (NCVQ) was founded. It was responsible for implementing the review of vocational qualifications (RVQ). In 1986, the UK Government was pursuing a rather isolationist policy in Europe; the RVQ focused intently on strategies designed to resolve the fundamental problems of a low level of training and an incoherent national qualification framework within England and Wales. These problems and deficits became more strongly evident during the implementation of the comparability exercise by Cedefop (Steedman and Wagner, 1998). The testimonies of key

---

[53] *Ministerie van Onderwijs, Ciltuur en Wetenschappen, Wet Educatie en Beroepsonderwijs; de Wet in hoofdlijnen*, Zoetermeer, 1996, p. 14.

policy-makers in 1986 and in 1998 confirmed this lack of commitment to articulation with EU structures and the tight focus on policy measures tailored to the situation in England and Wales.

Referring to EU systems, the report stated: '... Our remit is concerned with England and Wales and not with wider issues of the United Kingdom and the European Community. We have, however, taken note of the European Council decision of 16 July 1985, the aim of which is to assist mobility of labour within the Community by improving arrangements for recognition of comparability of vocational training qualifications between EU Member States. That decision referred to a five-level training structure. We have not addressed issues of comparability between that structure and our proposed framework. It is much too early to attempt any discussion of comparability' [54].

In practice, the level framework for England and Wales possessed a number of features that resulted in poor articulation with the EU structure. The problems to which these differences gave rise became particularly evident when effort was devoted to locating English qualifications in the EU framework during the mid-1990s. The differences between the framework endorsed by the RVQ and the EU framework can be summarised in two points.

First is the difference between a training orientation (EU) and an outcome orientation (NVQ framework). The Cedefop framework is based on training levels, whereas the NVQ levels are not related to formal training. NVQs are based on outputs and are intended to confirm that a person has successfully completed a series of nationally specified outcomes, irrespective of the mode, duration, or location of the learning. Second is the difference in emphasis on entry requirements (EU) and open access (NVQ framework). Part of the function of NVQs is to provide certification of workers who have developed skills over a period of time, through work rather than formal learning. Accreditation of prior learning/achievement is seen as an important requirement in the UK, which has had a comparatively low level of training. Thus, although in a few sectors, at particular levels, prerequisites are stated for certain units/qualifications, the NVQ criteria emphasise open access to units/qualifications. The NVQ levels framework is, therefore, not based on a 'route map' of what needs to be taken in order to progress to a higher level, nor on a necessary ladder of progression.

While the national framework is emphasised in national policy, and is a point of reference for organisations' policy and development work, a wide range of frameworks, such as the awarding body structures, continues to exist. Contrary

---

[54] RVQ, *Review of vocational qualifications,* Department of Education and Science and Manpower Services Commission, 1986. We have to remember that in 1986 the decision of 1985 on comparability had not yet been put into practice. The first results were published by 1987.

Table 5. **The 1985 European five-level framework and the 1997 Dutch five-level framework compared**

EUROPEAN FIVE-LEVEL FRAMEWORK	DUTCH QUALIFICATION FRAMEWORK
LEVEL 1 **Training that gives entry to this level: compulsory education and pre-vocational training.** This training is followed either in an educational establishment, or within the framework of extra-curricular training programmes, or in a company. The amount of theoretical knowledge and practical skill required is very limited. This qualification which is intended for carrying out fairly straightforward work, can be obtained fairly readily.	**LEVEL 1** **(Assistant)** An assistant is responsible for his/her own activities. Work consists primarily of the application of automated routines and (to a limited extent) the application of standard procedures. An assistant's work implies job-related skills and knowledge.
LEVEL 2 **Training that gives entry to this level: compulsory education and vocational training (including dual training as in apprenticeship schemes).** At this level, a full qualification is obtained for a clearly defined activity, using the instruments and techniques concerned. This activity consists largely of practical work, which can be carried out independently within the boundaries of techniques learned.	**LEVEL 2** **(Basic occupational practitioner)** A worker is responsible for his/her own activities. He/she and his/her colleagues share a collective responsibility for their work. A worker cooperates with colleagues. Work concentrates on applying automated routines and standard procedures implying occupation-related skills and knowledge.
LEVEL 3 **Training that gives entry to this level: compulsory education and/or vocational training and additional technical training or technical vocational training or other vocational training at secondary level.** This implies more theoretical knowledge than the previous level. This level mostly comprises practical work that can be carried out independently and/or comprises other responsibilities such as leadership and coordination.	**LEVEL 3** **(All-round practitioner)** A worker is responsible for his/her own activities and accounts for his/her actions to colleagues (non-hierarchical). A worker is responsible for monitoring and supervising the application of automated routines and standard procedures. Work concentrates on the application of standard procedures and combining these procedures. He/she combines or devises procedures for work preparation and supervisory activities. Work implies mainly occupational skills and knowledge.

EUROPEAN FIVE-LEVEL FRAMEWORK	DUTCH QUALIFICATION FRAMEWORK

LEVEL 4

Training that gives entry to this level: secondary vocational education (general or vocational training) and post-secondary technical training.
This is technical training at a higher level in educational establishments or elsewhere. The qualification obtained as a result of this training comprises knowledge and skills at a higher level, but in general terms does not require knowledge of scientific principles in the different areas concerned. These skills and knowledge make it possible, in particular, to take responsibility for planning and/or supervision and/or management in an autonomous or independent way.

LEVEL 4

(Specialist or middle manager)

A worker is responsible for the execution of his/her own work and has to account for his/her actions to colleagues (non-hierarchical). Additionally, he/she bears explicit hierarchical responsibility; this responsibility concerns planning and/or administration and/or management and/or development of a production cycle. Furthermore, he/she combines or devises new procedures. Work implies specialist skills and knowledge and/or transferral skills and knowledge.

LEVEL 5

Training that gives entry to this level: secondary education (general of vocational training) and full higher education.
Whoever has followed this training is able to carry out an occupational activity as a salaried or self-employed worker and has a thorough command of the scientific background of the occupation. The qualifications required for carrying out an occupational activity can be integrated at these various levels.

LEVEL 5

Training that gives entry to this level: secondary education (general of vocational training) and full higher education.
Whoever has followed this training is able to carry out an occupational activity as a salaried or self-employed worker and has a thorough command of the scientific background of the occupation. The qualifications required for carrying out an occupational activity can be integrated at these various levels.

to assumptions made by many researchers, the RVQ framework was not constructed with any deliberate reference to the EU levels.

Nowadays, there is scarce day-to-day reference to the EU levels, although researchers and actors familiar with Cedefop work and engaged with international comparative studies are aware of the framework and use it for comparative purposes. It does not, however, figure significantly in national policy discussions relating to the rationalisation or updating of the English qualifications system. In summary, neither from the point of competitiveness nor with regard to transparency can traces of the European five-level system be found in the English qualifications system.

8.6. Summary

From this analysis it appears that, of the countries involved in this project, only in Spain and the Netherlands has the European framework had a sustainable impact on post-1986 education reform. The definitions of the Spanish levels in vocational education were taken from the European five-level system and the introduction of level 1 in the Dutch secondary vocational qualification framework might have been inspired by this European system.

As a formal or substantive frame of reference for the (re)positioning of national systems, the European framework appears to have played no role in France, mainly because the French and European systems are roughly compatible. It played a very weak role in England, mainly limited to the issue of compiling national statistics that are comparable to those of other countries. For its part, England preferred to focus on measures tailored to improving skills flow into the economy, responding to a decline in traditional patterns of training. In the 1980s, policy sought to revitalise training through more flexible outcomes-based qualifications, dismantling the more formalised arrangements (apprenticeships, the industry training boards) in existence at that time.

The European five-level structure appeared in several national discussions. The European system has generated considerable resistance in Germany because the application of the criteria for allocation qualifications, in the view of that country, places too low a value on German apprenticeship schemes within secondary vocational education. However, this discussion did not lead to adjustment of either the German or the European system. In Spain, the desire to place secondary vocational education at a higher level in the European system led to the rephrasing of the definition of levels. The programmes of education and training were slightly adapted but not substantially changed. The Netherlands studied the European system and claims its new secondary vocational education four-level system is identical to the first four levels of the European five-level structure but this equalisation can hardly be justified from the criteria employed in both systems.

Finally, it is interesting, if not ironic, to note that English concepts on their part seem to inspire framework reforms in other European countries. The NVQ concept of uncoupling qualifications and (vocational) education programmes was adopted in the 1997 Dutch qualification framework. The equating principle of the 1998 national qualification framework has inspired Spain and France in proposing cohesive meta-frames of reference, encompassing the existing ones and intended to be valid for a wide range of (lifelong learning) purposes, clarifying the relative status of a great many qualifications to individuals and companies.

9. Conclusions

9.1. The scope of systems

The scope of national classification systems for vocational qualifications and standards is determined by three criteria:

(a) whether or not the application and use of the system is broader than for the identification and regulation of curricula and certificates of vocational education programmes;

(b) whether or not a system is a cohesive and comprehensive framework incorporating qualifications on a set of levels while these levels are defined coherently;

(c) whether or not the classification system is monopolistic in two senses: it comprises all qualifications that can be obtained and/or no other systems are in use.

None of the countries studied has a classification system consisting of one unique (monopolistic) set of qualifications serving as a reference frame to certify a wide variety of learning and work experience at an exhaustive range of levels. At the moment, England and France come closest, but do not meet the last criterion. Proposals now being discussed in Spain and France are coming close to meeting all criteria.

It is somewhat ironic to see that two English concepts seem to inspire continental framework reforms: the idea of uncoupling qualifications and (vocational) curricula and the introduction of a national 'framework of frameworks' encompassing different types of qualifications. The idea of uncoupling qualifications and vocational curricula was adopted in the 1997 Dutch qualification reform. The concept of a framework of frameworks seems to have inspired Spain and France in developing cohesive frames of reference that should connect the various existing provisions, whether they are education/training linked or employment linked, or whether they are based on initial VET or include non-formal or lifelong learning as well.

9.2. The definition of standards

Standards closely linked to (specific parts of) the educational/training domain were identified in four countries. This is quite clear in Germany and Spain where standards are incorporated into curricula or diplomas. In addition to the application of standards for educational purposes, France and the Netherlands use standards for the accreditation of prior learning (APL).

The new Spanish system will have a unified set of standards. The *SNC* will coordinate the development of standards for initial vocational education as well as for the training courses for job-seekers and will establish job descriptions at a supra-level. Even so, these standards are intended to serve as exit qualifications for all kinds of vocational education and training, whether initial or continuing in nature.

Only in English NVQs are the definitions of standards deliberately unrelated to formal education or training in schools, colleges or training centres. This was seen during the late 1980s and 1990s as a desirable means of encouraging an increase in the level of skills accredited (and developed) without regulating the location, duration and/or mode of learning. This was seen by the government of the day as a means of further 'rolling back the role of the State',increasing employer and employee responsibility for training and gaining qualifications and increasing the numbers gaining qualifications by increasing the ways in which it was possible to achieve them. The national framework of qualifications remains a framework for qualifications – it is not a curriculum specification. However, the importance of linking policy in qualifications, curriculum development, quality assurance of assessment and training, and increased funding is recognised by the DfEE and QCA.

Standards are supposed to define the characteristics of work in such a way that they are unambiguous and applicable to those supposed to work with them. Standards might serve a range of purposes. How do we define standards applicable for different settings? From the English example, we learn that with an increase in the number of purposes it is increasingly difficult to serve all purposes sufficiently. No satisfactory answer has yet been found to this question.

Another aspect for consideration is what characteristics of work should receive the most attention in standards. Should it be specific job requirements (the requirements of an occupation/profession) or current requirements of a given job (occupational requirements expected to be relevant in the future)? Do standards follow or set norms? All countries show evidence of trying to compromise between these possibilities. Most standards are supposed to cover skills and personal work experience acquired or to be obtained in work settings. At the same time, standards are supposed to ensure improvement (raise, broaden, prepare for the future) in the competence levels of learning and working individuals. This compromise leaves education and training with a problem. When courses are organised partly at school and partly in professional practice, vocational education is faced with a tension between the opportunities for practical training offered by businesses and the need to include future-oriented objectives in a programme.

9.3. The definition of qualifications

Qualifications are social constructs. This is obvious when we analyse debates on the division of qualifications into units and on the breadth of qualifications. Certainly, a classification system for qualifications becomes flexible by dividing qualifications into units. When parts of qualifications can be certified separately, it is possible to acquire a qualification over time or to have parts of one's work experiences certified. A greater variation in users' requirements can be answered. In being more flexible to individual needs, the certification of units can be considered to have its advantages. The question is, however, what roles are attributed to qualification frameworks? To which aims will all stakeholders feel committed? Are qualification frameworks intended to act as a frame of reference for individuals and/or companies assessing the currency of (lifelong) working and learning experiences? Or is a framework intended to stimulate young individuals to obtain a full qualification as a basis for lifetime employability? In this perspective, (a limited set of) units can never be allowed to substitute for a full qualification.

The fact that qualifications are social constructs is very visible in discussions on the breadth of qualifications. These debates focus on the issue of the extent to which a qualification should represent a specific occupation or job characteristics and to what extent qualifications should provide young and adult workers and learners with a broad (career) perspective. In most countries, several stakeholders participate in this debate on qualification definitions. It is, for instance, the strong belief of France and Spain that it is the role of the State to arbitrate between immediate individual (person and enterprise) interests and forward-looking global social interest. This explains why the State wants to be involved in the development of qualifications. In Germany, the social partners and the federal State share a long-standing consensus on the social status, and hence on the definition, of the *Ausbildungsberufe*.

In the Netherlands, this discussion will gain momentum in the very near future. The Ministry of Education's Advisory Committee on Qualifications (*ACOA*) developed a new competence-based framework for the definition of qualifications. At the end of 1999, it was still a concept but the general feeling is that this new framework will bind qualifications to initial vocational education even more closely, moving away from the interests of workers and enterprises. This is fuelling the discussion on whether initial vocational education and further (adult) training need separate systems and structures of qualification levels.

9.4. The levels in qualification frameworks

Qualification levels are defined differently in the various frameworks. Criteria used to identify levels can be divided into six groups:

1. input criteria or admission requirements for education and training programmes delivering qualifications or for the assessment of qualifications. For instance, (duration and type of) occupational experience or preliminary education or training;
2. characteristics of the programmes delivering qualifications. For instance, the programme duration or the learning venues;
3. output criteria in terms of learning outputs; the attainment goals;
4. output criteria in terms of occupational practice or the characteristics of work;
5. the position of a qualification in occupational hierarchies;
6. equation statements, formally stating the equality of qualifications at a certain level.

With the NVQs, England and Wales have a pure set of criteria as this framework only uses output criteria in terms of the characteristics of work (group 4), while the Dearing framework is an equating system in its purest form (group 6). French level criteria are used to define the level of diplomas and to determine the 'value' of study programmes and diplomas not belonging to the initial vocational education system. The principles behind the French classification of levels do not focus on the conditions of training but on the use that can be made of the levels of training in occupational practice. For this reason French level criteria can be labelled as group 5 criteria, indicating how diplomas are linked to occupational positions.

In all the other countries, a mixed set of qualifications is applied. German subsystem levels are defined by criteria taken from group 1 (*Weiterbildungsberufe*) and from groups 2 and 4. Descriptors taken from groups 2, 3 and 4 are used in Spain. For application in VET, the Dutch four-level framework uses criteria taken from groups 1, 2 and 5. Formally, only criteria taken from group

5 are used but, as Dutch qualifications are almost exclusively used to certify vocational education programmes, criteria taken from groups 1 and 2 are also applied.

Referring to this classification of level criteria, the 1985 European five-level structure (see Annex 2) uses criteria taken from groups 2, 3, 4 and 5 in a somewhat inconsistent way. Criteria taken from group 2 ('training that gives entry to this level') and from group 5 ('this activity consists largely of practical work, which can be carried out independently') can be found in the definition of all levels. Criteria from group 3 can be found in the definition of level 3 only ('this implies more theoretical knowledge...'), while criteria taken from group 4 can be found in the definition of levels 4 and 5 ('... has a thorough command of the scientific background of the occupation').

Basically, the ISCED-97 classification of education levels (see Annex 4) is unidimensional as the content of educational activities is the key to the level concept. Its overall level concept is defined in terms of the content of the underlying educational activities, and other criteria, for example starting ages, length of programmes, entrance conditions and qualification requirements, type of certificate, etc. A fundamental aspect of these criteria is that they complement, rather than exclude, each other. By definition, ISCED also covers vocational and professional education. Subject content rather than the intended occupation was chosen as a classification criterion for these types of education.

In France, the Netherlands and England, sectoral organisations develop qualifications for a range of levels. They also have the authority to allocate qualifications to levels though they tend not to use the typical characteristics of an occupation in this process but the characteristics of qualifications at the same or other levels. It becomes a reference process because the position proposed for a qualification is often determined more by its position relative to other qualifications, rather than by exact correspondence with the level descriptors. Sectoral organisations focus on the relative differences between the qualifications within their respective sectors. Since levels convey status – and present this in hierarchical form – the allocation of qualifications to levels can thus become subject to political and socio-cultural pressures.

9.5. Development and maintenance of standards and qualifications

With regard to the development and maintenance of standards and qualifications, the major differences between the countries in the report can be found in procedures assessing whether standards and qualifications should be revised and whether the newly produced standards and qualifications meet the criteria. Differences can be found particularly in the role of the State.

In England, France and the Netherlands, standing organisations are responsible for the maintenance of all sector-based qualifications. The English organisations are allowed to start an adjustment process only with the consent of a national organisation (QCA). The results of the development work must also be submitted to the QCA. This is also the case in France (the Ministry of Education) though far less so in the Netherlands where central management is virtually absent since the supervising *ACOA* committee does not have a strong position. In fact, sector-based bodies (*LOBs*) and higher professional education have a large degree of freedom in the development and establishment of standards and qualifications. The role of the State is restricted to the prior establishment of the criteria that all standards and qualifications must meet.

In contrast to England and the Netherlands, the French State is directly involved in the development of qualifications. Although the origin of a request for the creation of transformation of diplomas can be different sources, the Ministry of Education is directly involved in the process of developing diplomas. Ultimately, it is the ministry that decides. In Spain, too, qualifications are subject to political coordination as a national council composed of government representatives, social partners and regions supervises the development of all qualifications.

The fact that Germany has no comprehensive system is evident in the process of development of standards. With regard to the *Ausbildungsberufe*, broadly composed committees, in which the social partners and the government are represented, are established when a study programme plan is to be renewed. The social partners nominate experts in the actual job and also review the work of the experts. The study programme, however, complies with the criteria laid down by the federal government jointly with the *Länder* governments. Compared to the *Ausbildungsberufe*, the role of the social partners in the development of qualifications of *Weiterbildungsberufe* is even stronger but almost absent in the process of qualification development for the *Schulberufe.*

9.6. The impact of the European five-level system on national frameworks

Major reforms in qualification systems and structures have recently been implemented (England and Wales, the Netherlands) or are under discussion (France, Spain). In Germany, however, this applies only within higher education. In France and Spain, it is not the reform of the existing frameworks system that is being considered, it is the coherence between the various official qualification systems.

From our analysis, it appears that in Spain and the Netherlands the European system was taken into account in post-1986 reformations. The definitions of the Spanish levels in vocational education were taken from the European five-level system and the introduction of level 1 in Dutch secondary vocational qualifications might have been inspired by this European system.

In addition, the European five-level structure appeared in several national discussions. The European system has generated considerable resistance in Germany because the application of the European criteria, in the view of that country, places too low a value on German apprenticeship schemes within secondary vocational education. However, this resistance has not led to adjustment of either the German or the European system. In Spain, the desire to place secondary vocational education at a higher level in the European system led to the rephrasing of the definition of levels. The programmes of education and training were slightly adapted but not substantially changed. The Netherlands studied the European system and claims its new secondary vocational education four-level system is identical to the first four levels of the European five-level structure but this equalisation cannot be justified from the criteria employed in both systems.

As a formal or substantive frame of reference for the (re)positioning of the national systems, the European system appears to have played no role in France or England. The French and European systems are roughly compatible. England preferred to focus on policy measures tailored to the situation in England and Wales. The levels of the NVQ system (1985) deliberately veered away from any articulation with EU levels.

10. Towards a renewal of a European framework of qualification levels

The experiences of the European training and qualification levels structure, both within the Member States investigated and in European-level debates, are rather mixed and controversial. However, even if this structure was never legally binding, it had direct effects on some Member States' VET policy, and was broadly discussed and had indirect (slightly controversial) effects in the other Member States. In this final section, we try to summarise the experience.

10.1. The multiple functions of a framework

It is clear from our analysis of the aims of and developments in national classification systems and frameworks that these have different backgrounds and meanings in each country. Systems use different criteria and descriptors, or no formal descriptors at all. In fact, the choice of criteria and descriptors reflects the social and political aims that stakeholders wish to see realised by such a framework. The English Dearing system, for example, is meant as an instrument to impose a certain order within a qualification 'jungle'. The system is intended to be inclusive for many existing and quite heterogeneous qualifications that ought to be placed at the respective levels. Therefore, the system does not use descriptors as the basis for the framework but simply states that qualifications are equivalent and ought to be placed at the same level.

A further example comes from the Netherlands. New ideas were recently launched regarding the nature of qualifications in the Dutch secondary vocational education system. The argument for emphasising the necessity of new definitions was mainly that young people need to prepare for a lifetime career and not for a once-for-ever entry into a more or less narrow occupation. The 1997 Dutch definitions presented in this report cannot, however, be regarded as covering this issue properly. As a consequence, the newly defined qualifications do not intend only to convey actual occupational profiles but try to anticipate future developments as well.

Stakeholders' interests are expressed in the definition of standards, qualifications and levels and in the procedures for the development of standards and qualifications. Definitions and procedures express what stakeholders agree to be expressed in qualifications and in a classification of qualifications. In the end, qualifications are social constructs representing a consensus (which may be limited in time) between the interests of various stakeholders. Qualification systems are not neutral. A system does not represent reality in a simple way. This brings us to the conclusion that discussions concerning the character of qualifications and of level frameworks are not so much technical discussions but rather discussions on what a classification should express and for what purposes a framework for the classification of qualifications should be used. It ought be stated that a framework has different functions for different sets of stakeholders and interest groups and is politically constructed.

The most relevant functions and interest groups in this respect are:

(a) national policy-making, which aims to establish an accessible, coherent and transparent set of qualifications, creating continuous qualification pathways, guaranteeing (lifelong) rights of progress through, and access to, a qualification system, enhancing public quality assessment, harmonising existing qualifications or regulating the education and training provision/market;

(b) sectoral interests, which aim to keep education and training up to date with developments in job positions and occupations (in terms of content and occupational structures), establishing proper progression routes in terms of linked qualifications and diplomas, adapting particular education and training programmes to the needs of all segments of the sector, creating the grounds for an all-encompassing sector policy on education and training, etc.;

(c) statistical analysis and research, assisting researchers in analysing similarities and differences in educational performances within socio-economic sectors, on a national or international basis, rating qualifications or comparing hierarchies in qualifications and delivery;

(d) providing information for organisations and individuals wanting to assess the currency of qualifications: bodies or enterprises accepting qualifications for work or study, individuals wanting to identify qualifications relevant for future career opportunities or individuals wanting to assess the status of a qualification.

10.2. The dynamic of frameworks

Qualification frameworks are, by definition, reference systems. Frameworks establish relationships between teaching and learning outcomes and performances demanded by business and industry, on the one hand, and general or vocational qualifications and diplomas delivered by a given education or training system on the other. Qualification frameworks aim to make relationships between qualifications more transparent, as well as clarifying major differences between them. The major challenge of a qualification framework, therefore, is that it should be both transparent and relevant in terms of coping with the expectations of all stakeholders and interest groups. Meeting both ends and serving the individual employers and employees are apparently far from easy. Either a framework aims to cover a great variety of qualifications by simply equating them and allowing all existing qualifications to be included in one comprehensive framework (England and Wales, the new French and Spanish concepts) or a framework limits itself to a criteria-based representation of qualifications in one or more segments of the respective national education system (the Dutch, German and the current Spanish frameworks). The forthcoming framework in Spain, however, seems to be very much in line with the European framework.

Establishing transparent and relevant relationships between qualifications within a framework will be even more difficult. The second article of the Council decision on the five-level system states: 'the Commission, in close cooperation between the Member States, shall undertake work to fulfil the aims set out in Article 1 on the comparability of vocational training qualifications between the various Member States, in respect of specific occupations or groups of occupations (55)'. It might be concluded from this quote that a close, if not direct, relationship between education and training certificates and job positions was assumed to exist in 1985. Is this still the case? All national frameworks are currently, and will presumably continue to be, under discussion in terms of how robust they are and how capable they are of coping with accelerated changes in both education and employment. All qualification frameworks are challenged by developments in the subsystems to which they are supposed to relate.

Frameworks have to respond to developments such as:
(a) increasing pressure on established and supra-workplace definitions of occupations. Traditionally, a qualification represents one or more distinct occupations. Decentralisation of wage negotiations, frequent changes in the organisation of production processes and increasing shop-floor

---

(55) Council Decision 85/368/EEC of 16 July 1985 on the comparability of vocational training qualifications between the Member States of the European Union.

autonomy question current definitions of occupations. The German *Berufsprinzip,* for instance, is currently coming under great pressure and runs the risk of becoming an isolated exception to this phenomenon. Hence, occupational profiles and occupation-based qualifications seem to ask: 'Do we really want to be so cautious? Aren't we sure that they are losing ground?'. What does this mean for the definition of levels and the definition of qualifications?

(b) the proliferation of teaching and learning places or outcomes. Developments in tertiary education, described in Section 7 and in Heitmann's contribution hereunder, are a good example of this phenomenon. More generally, developments in work-based learning, in continuing education and training and lifelong learning, and organisation development challenge (see below) the monopoly of school and initial training. Learning becomes more open in terms of problem solving and developing new work methods and processes. There are no answers yet to how the outcomes of these open-ended learning processes can properly be defined in terms of standards and made transparent in view of an identification of a comprehensive and discriminating set of levels;

(c) the reassessment of the position of initial (vocational) education and its impact on standards. The necessity of lifelong learning, the increasing pressure on an individual to keep up with change and to stay employable for life, will challenge (see below) the traditional function of initial education. Initial education should no longer prepare for a once-for-ever entry into an occupation but for lifetime employability. In some countries, for instance in the Netherlands, the lifelong learning debate is moving towards the redefinition of initial vocational education and training standards. Such standards, however, should not establish a close link to the labour market but should be more integrated with general education, offering a broad basis for a lifetime career, thus closing the gap between the aim of initial and continuous education The need for rearrangements in the balance between initial and post-initial education is discussed from the perspective of lifelong learning; not all education should be concentrated in somebody's youth. How can this be rationalised with using one and the same set of vocational standards and qualifications for the assessment of both initial and post-initial teaching and learning?

Stakeholders need to agree on the aims and coverage of frameworks, which ought to take into account these developments. This is because, in most cases, several interest groups must share the feeling of ownership: the use of a framework is not limited to one single purpose. Furthermore, these developments are hardly, if at all, covered in today's definitions of standards, qualifications and qualification levels. The current Dutch, French, German and Spanish concepts are still too closely linked to (initial secondary) vocational education programming, while an equating meta-framework has no impact on existing qualifications and procedures. It leaves the answers to these questions to the bodies producing qualifications, allowing them to come up with their own answers. In the end, this policy will devalue the frameworks' transparency and relevance for political, statistical and information purposes. More recent developments in Spain and the UK, however, may indicate the direction to take.

10.3. Time for a new European initiative?

What do these reflections mean for a European framework of qualifications? With the publication of the updated ISCED-97 manual in 1999, the position of the 1985 European five-level system has become disputable: are two frameworks necessary, and, if so, on what grounds should the 1985 five-level system be updated? In any debate on frameworks at European level, both the following points are relevant.

First, the definitions, the number of levels and the procedures for producing qualifications reflect the aims of a framework. Any framework is a product of the relative influence of stakeholders such as the State, economic sectors, social partners, individual enterprises, or the actors within the education system. A framework expresses their aims and purposes. Different aims will lead to different frameworks; no universal framework exists.

Second, frameworks are not static and are not developed for eternity. Frameworks of qualifications establish relationships between moving targets. They link dynamic entities such as teaching and learning outcomes, performances demanded by business and industry, vocational qualifications or diplomas, and general and vocational segments of a national education system. Structural and conceptual changes in one of these entities do not necessarily have an impact on frameworks.

The 1999 revision of the ISCED-97 framework has its foundation in traditional (initial) education systems and programmes. Descriptors such as entry ages, entry requirements and programme duration are no longer relevant in an age of increasing programme flexibility, proliferation of teaching and learning venues, and outcomes, and growing efforts for lifelong learning ([56]).

([56]) The level concept of the 1999 edition of ISCED is based on the content of the underlying education activities, using auxiliary criteria such as starting ages of participants, duration of programmes, entrance qualifications, and types of subsequent education for which those who complete the activities are eligible (the 1999 manual, pp. 9–13).

The1999 framework does not take sufficiently into account new developments in teaching and learning and in vocational education. In other words, there is no international or European framework yet that meets all the criteria identified in this section.

The first point in defining basic concepts for a European framework is the identification of purposes: policy-making, serving sectoral interests, statistical analysis and research, and providing information. Sellin's observation that 'education and vocational training systems and the bureaucracies seem to resist with all their might any influences in connection with a "Europeanisation" of their structures' ([57]) implies that a European consensus on the renewal of the 1985 five-level system, trying to compare qualifications between all present and future Member States, will be hard to obtain as long as common purposes are not clearly identified. The 1985 framework did not succeed in clarifying these purposes prior to its implementation. Each Member State identified its purpose and anticipated its impact differently. This is made clear by the analysis in this report, showing the quite different impact this framework had, for instance, in England, France and Germany in particular. In other words, there seems to be no broad consensus on the introduction of a European framework which could serve wider European Union policy intentions in education, training and employment. There exist, undoubtedly, objective needs in line with purposes linked to European labour mobility and teacher, pupil or trainee exchanges within Europe.

If a common European social and employment policy were in place, then a closer cooperation in education and training matters would impose itself. However, as long as these policies are insufficiently high on the European agenda, a common understanding on qualifications, levels and frameworks does not impose itself.

Focus on a special interest may include the social partners within the European-level social dialogue and more especially certain branches and sectors within the sector-level dialogue, for example construction industries, transport and agriculture. In addition, such a framework may deliver clear indicators for statistical analyses and research, providing comparable information, for instance, to support the efforts of the Member States to implement action plans on employment within a common European employment strategy and guidelines. Bigger European companies (and their social partners) may also have a special interest in such a transparency of training levels, especially if they have a European works council.

---

[57] Sellin, B., `Do joint European vocational training standards stand a chance?´, discussion paper in Cedefop–Panorama, Thessaloniki, February 1996.

It seems that no easy solution in terms of an adequate basic concept is available. Perhaps we should not look for such a basic concept as a starting point for discussion and should not focus on a revival of the 1985 framework in the short term. There are quite a few arguments in favour of a more fundamental rethinking of qualification frameworks, providing there is a consensus on the aims and purposes of such a European framework. In fact, the main arguments have already been identified in this section:

(a) the need to rethink the impact of blurring demarcations between occupations;
(b) the growing flexibility of educational and training programmes and provisions;
(c) the proliferation of teaching and learning venues and outcomes;
(d) the definition of hierarchies in competences in relation to both learning outcomes and company-based definitions of knowledge;
(e) the need for a comprehensive level reference framework for learning pathways throughout somebody's lifetime;
(f) the widening of the set of (personal) skills demanded in business and industry (identity regulation, according to Alvesson) [58].

These topics should be reflected in the definition of levels, standards and qualifications. The analysis of the five Member States and their approach to level frameworks, however, seems to underline a general need for establishing such frameworks at least on the national level in order to ensure transparency and coherence. This trend may well, in the medium term, lead to a new European initiative. The issue is not so much whether a new European initiative is or is not required. It is whether the same general need will be perceived at European level.

European platforms might take the initiative to start this debate and study the impact of these developments on levels, standards and qualifications. While it is true that the product of such a project will not be the launching of a ready-made framework, the outcome will surely feed many debates about a new generation of (inter)national frameworks, capable of coping with a great variety of structural and conceptual changes in work, teaching and learning.

---

[58] Alvesson, M., *Knowledge work: ambiguity, image and identity,* University of Lund, Sweden, 1998.

Annexes

Annex 1. References

For this report

Alvesson, M., *Knowledge work: ambiguity, image and identity,* University of Lund, Sweden, 1998.

Cedefop, Andersson, R. and Olsson, A., *Development of an internationally comparable classification for fields of vocational education and training,* Thessaloniki and Eurostat. Luxembourg, 1999.

Cedefop, Sellin, B., *Anticipation of trends in occupations and qualifications,* published in www.trainingvillage.gr/etv/ as 2000 PDF file.

Cedefop, Sellin, B., *Do common European training standards stand a chance?,* Thessaloniki, 1997.

Cedefop, Sellin, B., *European trends in the development of occupations and qualifications,* Volume II, Thessaloniki, 1999.

DTI, *The impact on vocational training of studies analysing and forecasting trends in occupations,* Cedefop document, 1998.

NetreF, *A network of national reference structures for vocational qualifications: summary report results,* COLO, 1998.

OECD, *Classifying educational programmes,* manual for ISCED-97 implementation, 1999 edition.

Scherer, W., *Transparenz beruflicher Befähigungsnachweise in Europa,* Cedefop, Thessaloniki, 1997.

Streumer, W. et al., *Richtlijnen voor het formuleren van eindtermen,* CINOP, 's-Hertogenbosch, 1996.

For Germany

Adler, T.and Benner, H., '*Regelung der Berufsausbildung in der Bundesrepublik Deutschland'Ausbildungsberufe im Wandel,* Bundesinstitut für Berufsbildung, Der Generalsekretär (ed.), Ergebnisse, Veröffentlichungen und Materialien aus dem BIBB, xeroxed manuscript, 1995.

Benner, H., *Ordnung der staatlich anerkannten Ausbildungsberufe,* Bundesinstitut für Berufsbildung, Der Generalsekretär (ed.), Bielefeld, 1995.

BMBF (1997) (Federal Ministry of Education and Research): *Reformprojekt Berufliche Bildung,* xeroxed manuscript, Berlin and Bonn, 1997.

Bundesinstitut für Berufsbildung, Der Generalsekretär (ed.), *Weiterbildungsberufe-Berufe mit Zukunft,* Ergebnisse, Veröffentlichungen und Materialien aus dem BIBB, Berlin, xeroxed manuscript, Berlin and Bonn, 1992.

Bundesinstitut für Berufsbildung. Der Generalsekretär(ed.) *Vorlage zur Sitzung 3/95 des Unterausschusses 2 - Strukturfragen der beruflichen Bildung* - am 22. November 1995 in Bonn, Top 3 - Beratungsvorlage zu dem Thema Gesundheitsberufe, xeroxed manuscript, 1995.

Bundesinstitut für Berufsbildung, Der Generalsekretär (ed.), *Entwicklungschancen durch Weiterbildung: Weiterbildung und Alternativen*, Ergebnisse, Veröffentlichungen und Materialien aus dem BIBB, Berlin and Bonn, 1996.

Bundesinstitut für Berufsbildung, Der Generalsekretär (ed.), *Vorlage zur Beschlußfassung zur Sitzung 1/99 des Hauptausschusses am 18./19,* März 1999 in Bonn, xeroxed manuscript, 1999.

Bundesausschuß für Berufsbildung, Empfehlungen über Kriterien und Verfahren für den Erlaß von Weiterbildungsordnungen und deren Gliederung, *Berufsbildung in Wissenschaft und Praxis*, No 2, 1976, pp. 4-5.

Bundesinstitut für Berufsbildung, 'Kriterien der Arbeitgeber vom Januar 1997 und der Gewerkschaften von November 1996', *Vorlage für den Hauptausschuß* vom 19.2.1997, 1997.

Collingro, P., Heitmann, G. and Schild, H., *Identifizierung, Bewertung und Anerkennung von früher und informell erworbenen Kenntnissen - Deutschland*, Cedefop, Thessaloniki, 1997.

Finegold, D. and Keltner, B., '*A cross-national perspective on skill standards systems*', conference paper, 1997.

Hecker, U., '*Lehrgänge zur Vorbereitung auf die Externenprüfung* - Unterstützung beim nachträglichen Erwerb des Berufsabschlusses', *Berufsbildung in Wissenschaft und Praxis*, Vol. 22, No 3, 1993, pp. 32-37.

Hoch, H.D., *Generalisten oder Spezialisten - Neue Portraits für die Bauberufe* - Referat auf den Hochschultagen Berufliche Bildung am 23. September 1998 in Dresden, manuscript, 1999.

KMK (1992) (Secretariat of the Standing Conference of Ministers for Education of the Federal States of the Federal Republic of Germany), *Rahmenvereinbarung über die Ausbildung und Prüfung zum technischen Assistenten/zur technischen Assistentin an Berufsfachschulen* vom 12.6.1992, version dated 26.6.1998.

KMK (1997a) (Secretariat of the Standing Conference of Ministers for Education of the Federal States of the Federal Republic of Germany), *Handreichungen für die Erarbeitung von Rahmenlehrplänen der Kultusministerkonferenz für den berufsbezogenen Unterricht in der Berufsschule und ihre Abstimmung mit Ausbildungsordnungen des Bundes für anerkannte Ausbildungsberufe*, Bonn, xeroxed manuscript, version dated 12.6.1997.

KMK (1997b) (Secretariat of the Standing Conference of Ministers for Education of the Federal States of the Federal Republic of Germany), '*Rahmenvereinbarung über die Berufsfachschulen*' (Beschluß der Kultusministerkonferenz vom 28.2.1997), in *Berufsbildung*, No 45/1997 pp. 43-47.

KMK (1998) (Secretariat of the Standing Conference of Ministers for Education of the Federal States of the Federal Republic of Germany*),' Rahmenvereinbarung über Fachschulen mit zweijähriger Ausbildungsdauer'* (Beschluß der Kultusministerkonferenz vom 12.6.1992 in der Fassung vom 2.10.1998), Bonn, xeroxed manuscript.

Koch, R., *Fünf-Stufen-Schema der EG von 1985 - Untersuchung über Auswirkungen der Zuordnung deutscher Berufsabschlüsse*, Institut der Deutschen Wirtschaft, Cologne, xeroxed manuscript, 1995.

Letzner, S. and Tillmann, H., '*Die Weiterbildungsregelungen der zuständigen Stellen*', *Ordnungsstruktur und Entwicklungstendenzen,* Bundesinstitut für Berufsbildung, Der Generalsekretär (ed.), Wissenschaftliches Diskussionspapier, No 33, Berlin and Bonn, 1998.

Marek, S. and Neumann, K.-H., *Qualifikationsangebote über berufliche Vollzeitschulen und Berufsakademien*, Teil I: Berufsfachschulen, Arbeitsgemeinschaft für angewandte Sozialforschung, Munich, xeroxed manuscript, 1999.

Meifort, B., *Warum ein BBiG-geregelter Pflegeberuf? Argumente für die Übernahme des dualen Systems in die Berufsbildung der Gesundheits- und Sozialpflege*, 1998.

Mettin, G., Gesundheitspflegerin/Gesundheitspfleger – *Überlegungen zu einem neuen Berufsbild für die Pflege nach BBiG*, Bundesinstitut für Berufsbildung, Der Generalsekretär (ed.), Bielefeld.

Meifort, B., *Probleme der Verrechtlichung der Berufsbildung für Berufe im Gesundheits- und Sozialwesen, in Bundesinstitut für Berufsbildung*, Der Generalsekretär (ed.), *Berufsbildung und Beschäftigung im personenbezogenen Dienstleistungssektor,* Wissenschaftliche Diskussionspapiere, Berlin, 1999.

Meifort, B.and Mettin, G. *Gesundheitspflegerin/Gesundheitspfleger – Überlegungen zu einem neuen Berufsbild für die Pflege nach BBiG*, Bundesinstitut für Berufsbildung, Der Generalsekretär (ed.), Bielefeld 1998.

Scholz, D. '*Meisterregelungen', in Cramer, G. et al. Ausbilder-Handbuch,* Abschnitt 5.10.3, Cologne, 1996, p. 4.

Stiller, I. '*Verfahren zur Erstellung von Ausbildungsordnungen'*, in Cramer, G. et al. *Ausbilder-Handbuch,* Abschnitt 9.3.2, Cologne, 1995.

Tillmann, H. '*Steuerung und Regelung der beruflichen Weiterbildung'*, Kurseinheit 2, Steuern und Regeln beruflicher Weiterbildung im Rahmen des Berufsbildungsgesetzes (BBiG), Fernuniversität Gesamthochschule in Hagen, 1989.

Tillmann, H. '*Weiterbildungsregelungen der Zuständigen Stellen'* in Cramer, G. et al. *Ausbilder-Handbuch,* Abschnitt 5.10.1, Cologne, 1995, p. 4.

Tillmann, H. '*Weiterbildungsregelungen des Bundes'*, in Cramer, G. et al. *Ausbilder-Handbuch*, Abschnitt 5.10.1, Cologne, 1995, p. 4.

For Spain

Acuerdo sobre Cobertura de Vac_os, Resolution of 13 May 1997.

De Pablo, A., '*La nueva formaci_n profesional: Dificultades de una construcci_n'*, REIS 77-78, Madrid, 1997, p.156.

Del Rey Guanter, S., '*La negociaci_n colectiva tras la reforma laboral de 1994. Perspectivas a la luz de los acuerdos colectivos de 1997'*, Estudios, 62, Consejo Econ_mico y Social, Madrid, 1998.

INEM, '*Plan de actuaci_n para la actualizaci_n de la formaci_n profesional. Estudios sectoriales de necesidades de formaci_n'*, Madrid.

Manzanares, J., '*El conocimiento de las cualificaciones en Espa_a y su optimizaci_n'*, Revista de Econom_a y Sociolog_a, 21 and 22 Madrid, 1993.

Manzanares, J., '*Cualificaci_n, formaci_n y clasificaci_n profesional. Notas para un debate'*, Herramientas, 53, Madrid, 1999.

MEC '*White Paper on the reform of the education system'* Madrid, 1989.

Moreno Pi_ero, F. and Parra Abad, E., '*Clasificaci_n professional y Movilidad'*, Revista de Econom_a y Sociolog_a, 21 and 22 Madrid, 1993.

Prieto, C. and Homs, O., '*Formation, emploi et compétitivité en Espagne'*,. Sociologie du Travail, 4 pp. 557-575.

For France

Affichard, J., '*Nomenclatures de formation et pratiques de classement*', *Formation Emploi*, No 4, October-December, 1983, pp. 47-61.

Commissariat général du plan d'équipement et de productivité, *V plan 1966-1970, Rapport général de la Commission de la main-d'œuvre*, 1966.

Conseil national de l'information statistique, '*Nomenclature des spécialités de formation – Guide d'utilisation*', Journal officiel, Paris, 1994.

Fourastié, J., '*Image de la population active en 1975 selon le niveau de qualification*', *Population*, July-September,1963.

Vimont, C. and Dubrulle, N., '*La prévision de l'emploi dans le cadre du V plan en France, 2 partie: essai de calcul des besoins de recrutement par niveau et type de formation*', *Population*, September-October, 1966.

For the Netherlands

ACOA, *De ontwikkeling van de kwalificatiestructuur voor het secundaire beroepsonderwijs: een tussenstand (discussienota)*, ACOA, 1996.

ACOA, *1 Verder aan het werk met de WEB, de ontwikkeling van de kwalificatiestructuur voor secundair beroepsonderwijs*, ACOA, 1997.

Blokhuis, F. and van Zolingen, S., *De kern te pakken: sleutelkwalificaties, kernproblemen en de landelijke kwalificatiestructuur*, CINOP/Universiteit Twente, 1997.

Blokhuis, F. and Klarus R., *Accreditation of prior learning in the Netherlands*, CINOP, 1997.

CBS, *Standaard onderwijsindeling*, editie 1998/1999, CBS 1999.

Commissie herijking kwalificatiestructuur, *Kwalificatiestructuur secundair beroepsonderwijs: advies van de commissie herijking kwalificatiestructuur*, 1995.

ISCED, *International standard classification of education*, Unesco, 1997.

Ministerie van Onderwijs, Cultur en Wetenschappen, *WEB, de wet educatie beroepsonderwijs, de kwalificatiestructuur beroepsonderwijs*, 1996.

Ministerie van Onderwijs, Cultur en Wetenschappen, *Formaat kwalificatiestructuur, het indelingsschema van de kwalificatiestructuur secundair beroepsonderwijs*, 1994.

Ministerie van Onderwijs, Cultur en Wetenschappen, HOOP, *Ontwerp Hoger Onderwijs en Onderzoek Plan 1998*, 1997.

Ministerie van Onderwijs, Cultur en Wetenschappen, *Ontwerp Hoger Onderwijs en Onderzoek Plan 2000*, Zoetermeer, 1999.

Mechelen, R. P. M. van, *Vergelijkend onderzoek eindtermen, vestigingskwalificaties en WEB-kwalificaties, eindrapportage BVE Raad*, CINOP, 1997.

Meteren, J., *Kwalificatiestructuur en infrastructuur, casus verzorging en verpleging*, CINOP, 1998.

Nafzger, J., *Reconstructie format voor kwalificatiestructuren*, CINOP, 1997.

Swager, R., Getuigen van niveau, de niveauclassificatie verduidelijkt, CIBB(CINOP), 1995/1996.

Vereniging van Hogescholen, *Niet meer maar beter, verslag van de commissie referentiekader onderwijsaanbod*, The Hague, 1995.

Visser, K., F. Blokhuis, R. Klarus (eds.), *Jaarboek kwalificatiestructuur*, CINOP,1998.

Visser, K., *Beroepsonderwijs en scholing in Nederland*, CIBB, 1992.

Visser, K., *Systems and procedures of certification of qualifications in the Nether*

For the United Kingdom (England and Wales)

Adey, P. and Yates, C., *Better learning – A report from the cognitive acceleration in science education project,* Kings College, London, 1990.

Archer, M., *The social origins of education systems,* Sage, 1979.

Boaler, J., *How valuable is international test success?* King's College, London, 1996.

CBI, *Towards a skills revolution,* Confederation of British Industry, 1989.

BSA, *The literacy and numeracy of adults,* Basic Skills Agency, 1995.

Dearing, R., *Review of the national curriculum,* Schools Curriculum and Assessment Authority, 1994.

Dearing, R., *The review of qualifications for 16-19 year-olds,* Schools Curriculum and Assessment Authority, 1996.

DES and ED, *Working together - Education and training,* HMSO, 1986.

Eraut, M., *Developing professional knowledge and competence*, Falmer Press, 1994.

Finegold, D. and Soskice, D., '*The failure of training in Britain: an analysis and prescription',* Oxford Review of Economic Policy, Vol No 2, *1988,* pp 21-53.

Finegold, D., '*Institutional incentives and skill creation: preconditions for a high-skill equilibrium'* in Ryan P. (1991), *International comparisons of vocational education and training for intermediate skills,* Falmer Press, 1991.

Fitzgibbon, C. et al., *Learning styles in GNVQs,* National Council for Vocational Qualifications, 1997.

Green, A., *Education and state formation*, Macmillan, 1991.

Green, A., *Education, globalisation and the nation state,* Macmillan, 1997.

Hart, K. et al, *Mathematical Understanding in children 5-16,* Macmillan, 1979.

Hyland, T., *Competence, education and NVQs – Dissenting perspectives*, Cassell Education, 1994.

Jessup, G., *Outcomes: NVQs and the emerging model of education and training,* Falmer Press, 1991.

Mansfield, R. and Mathews, D., *Job competence,* Further Education Staff College, 1985.

MSC, *NTI – A new training initiative,* Manpower Services Commission.

Nacett, *National education and training targets,* National Council for Education and Training Targets.

Nickell, S. and Bell, B., '*The collapse in demand for the unskilled and unemployed across the OECD',* Oxford Review of Economic Policy, Vol. 11, No 1, 1995.

Oates, T., *The RVQ levels,* Further Education Staff College, 1986.

Oates, T., *Developing and piloting the NCVQ key skills units,* National Council for Vocational Qualifications, 1991.

Oates, T., '*Core skills and transfer – Aiming high',* in Educational and Training Technology International Vol. 29, No 3, Kogan Page, 1992.

Oates, T., *A converging system? Explaining difference in the academic and vocational tracks in England and Wales,* Center on Education and Training for Employment, Ohio State University, Columbus, Ohio, 1995.

Oates, T., *The development and implementation of key skills in England and Wales*, National Council for Vocational Qualifications, 1996.

Oates, T. and Fettes, P., *Key skills strategy paper,* Qualifications and Curriculum Authority, 1998.

Oates, T., *Analysing and describing competence – Critical perspectives,* Qualifications and Assessment Authority, 1999.

Oates, T., *An analysis of the implementation of levels frameworks in the English education and training system 1986 to 1999*, Qualifications and Curriculum Authority, 2000.

Pirie, S., *'Calculating the risks', Nursing Standard 1984*, 12 July, 1984.

Reuling, J. *'Beruf princip'*, paper to the third International Conference of Learning at Work, Milan, June 1994.

Robinson, P., *Education, training and the youth labour market*, Institute for Public Policy Research, 1998.

Ryan, P., *'Initial training, labour market structure and public policy: intermediate skills in British and German industry'* in Ryan P. (1991), *International comparisons of vocational education and training for intermediate skills*, Falmer Press, 1991.

RVQ, *Review of vocational qualifications*, Department of Education and Science and Manpower Services Commission, 1986.

Sellin, B., *Comparability of vocational training levels*, Cedefop, Vocational Training, 1985.

Tapper, T. and Salter, B., *Education and the political order*, Macmillan, 1978.

Tapper, T. and Salter B., *Education, politics and the state*, Macmillan, 1981.

Senker, P., *'The relationship of the NVQ system to learning in the workplace'*, paper to the conference, 'The certification of vocational qualifications in France and the United Kingdom', CEREQ, Marseilles, March 2000.

Steedman, H., *Apprenticeship – A strategy for growth*, London School of Economics, Centre for Economic Performance, 1998.

Wilmott, A. and Cresswell, M., *Levels in national curriculum assessment*, Schools Examinations and Assessment Council, 1988.

Wilson, P., *Lifelong learning – Developing qualifications to support lifelong learners*, National Institute for Adult and Continuing Education, 1999.

Wolf, A., *Learning in context – Patterns of skill transfer and their learning implications* Training Agency, 1989.

Wolf, A., *'Assessing key skills – Wisdom or wild goose chase?'*, Cambridge Journal of Education, 189-201, 1991.

Qualification Level Structures in tertiary education

Berghe, Van den, W., *'Indikatoren aus verschiedenen Perspektiven', Die Anwendung von Qualitätsindikatoren in der beruflichen Bildung und Ausbildung*, Cedefop, Document, Thessaloniki, 1998.

Björnavold, J. *'Assessment of non-formal learning: the quality and limitations of methodologies'*, Vocational Training, No 12, European Journal, 1998.

BMBF, Bundesministerium für Bildung, Wissenschaft, Forschung und Technologie, *Äquivalenzen im Hochschulbereich*, Bonn, 1996.

Cedefop-Panorama, Systeme und Verfahren der Zertifizierung von Qualifikationen in der Europäischen Gemeinschaft, Thessaloniki, July 1993.

Commission de titres d'ingenieur (CTI), *References and orientations*, Paris, 1998.

Council of Europe/Unesco, Convention on the Recognition of Qualifications concerning higher education in the European region, Lisbon, 11.4.1997, for details: *Explanatory report to the convention*.

Dutch Validation Council (DVC), *Manual for the validation of master courses*, 1998.

European Ministers for Education, *'The European higher education area, Joint declaration of the European Ministers for Education'*, convened in Bologna, 19 June 1999.

Hochschulrahmengesetz (HRG), in der Fassung vom 20.8.1998, ¨ 19.

Hochschulrektorenkonferenz (HRK), 1999, die HRK hat eine von den Hochschulen abrufbare und leicht einsetzbare *Software zur Einführung des 'Diploma Supplement'* entwickelt, Bonn, HRK-Pressemitteilung vom 10.11.1999.

Jablonska-Skinder, H. and Teichler, U., '*Handbook of Higher Education Diplomas* in Europe', Saur, Munich 1992.

'*Joint declaration on the harmonisation of the architecture of the European higher education system',* 25 May 1998, by the four ministers in charge for Germany, France, Italy and the United Kingdom, Paris, the Sorbonne..

Kultusministerkonferenz (KMK), '*Vereinbarung der Kultusministerkonferenz der Fachrichtungen',* Studiengänge und Diplomgrade an Fachhochschulen. Bonn, 1996, Beschluß der KMK vom 20.10.1996.

National Committee of Inquiry into Higher Education (NCIHE) *Education in the learning society*, the Dearing report, HMSO, London, 1997.

OECD, *Education at a glance*, OECD indicators, Paris,1998.

OECD, *Redefining tertiary education*, Paris, 1998.

QAA, Quality Assurance Agency for Higher Education, (1999), '*The way ahead'*, Higher Quality, Bulletin of the QAA, 4 October 1999.

QAA, '*A consultative paper on higher education qualifications frameworks for England, Wales and Northern Ireland (EWNI), and for Scotland',* 1999.

Sellin, B., 'Do joint European vocational training standards stand a chance?', discussion paper, *Cedefop-Panorama*, Thessaloniki, February 1996.

Teichler, U., *Studieren bald 50 % eines Geburtsjahrgangs? Hochschulwesen*, 4/99, 1999, pp. 114-119.

Vroeijenstijn, A. I., '*External quality assessment in the Netherlands: the third generation'*, Utrecht, contribution to the first European Workshop on Assessment of Engineering Education Programmes (EWAEP 1), Gent, 1998.

The European five-level framework

Council Decision
of 16 July 1985

on the comparability of vocational training qualifications between the Member States of the European Community (85/368/EEC)

The Council of the European Communities

Having regard to the Treaty establishing the European Economic Community, and in particular Article 128 thereof,

Having regard to Council Decision 63/266/EEC of 2 April 1963 laying down general principles for implementing a common vocational training policy ([1]), and in particular the eighth principle thereof,

Having regard to the proposal from the Commission, as amended on 17 July 1984,

Having regard to the opinion of the European Parliament ([2]),

Having regard to the opinion of the Economic and Social Committee ([3]),

Whereas the eighth principle of Decision 63/266/EEC is to make it possible to achieve the mutual recognition of certificates and other documents confirming completion of vocational training;

Whereas the Council resolution of 6 June 1974 ([4]) on the mutual recognition of diplomas, certificates and other evidence of formal qualifications requires lists of such qualifications recognised as being equivalent to be drawn up;

Whereas the absence of the said mutual recognition is a factor inhibiting freedom of movement for workers within the Community, in so far as it restricts the possibility for workers seeking employment in one Member State to rely on vocational qualifications which they have obtained in another Member State;

Whereas there is a very substantial degree of diversity in the vocational training systems in the Community; whereas these systems are constantly requiring adaptation to the new situations brought about by the impact of technological change on employment and job content;

Whereas the Council resolution of 11 July 1983 concerning vocational training policies in the European Community in the 1980s ([5]) affirmed the need for a convergence of policies in the vocational training field, whilst recognising the diversity of training systems in the Member States, and the need for Community action to be flexible;

Whereas it has been possible for the Commission to establish as a reference point, with the help of the Advisory Committee for Vocational Training, a structure of levels of training which represents a first step towards the achievement of the aims laid down in the eighth principle of Decision 63/266/EEC, but whereas this structure does not reflect all the training systems being developed in the Member States;

Whereas for the skilled-worker level within this structure, and for selected priority groups of occupations, it has been possible to arrive at practical job descriptions and to identify the corresponding vocational training qualifications in the various Member States;

Whereas consultation with the vocational sectors concerned has provided evidence that these results can provide firms, workers and public authorities with valuable information concerning the comparability of vocational training qualifications;

Whereas the same basic methodology could be applied to other occupations or groups of occupations on advice from the Advisory Committee for Vocational Training and with the collaboration of employers, workers and the public authorities in the vocational sectors concerned;

Whereas it is therefore essential to make rapid progress towards the comparability of vocational training qualifications for all skilled workers, and to extend the work to other levels of training as quickly as possible;

Whereas it is advisable to have all the necessary opinions, in particular that of the Advisory Committee for Vocational Training, and the technical assistance of the European Centre for the Development of Vocational Training, and to enable the Member States and the Commission to act in accordance with existing procedures;

Whereas the Advisory Committee for Vocational Training delivered an opinion at its meeting on 18 and 19 January 1983;

Whereas paragraph 21 of the report of the Committee on a People's Europe of 29 and 30 March 1985 should be taken into account,

Has adopted this decision

ARTICLE 1

The aim of enabling workers to make better use of their qualifications, in particular for the purposes of obtaining suitable employment in another Member State, shall require, for features of job descriptions mutually agreed by the Member States on behalf of workers, within the meaning of Article 128 of the Treaty, expedited common action by the Member States and the Commission to establish the comparability of vocational training qualifications in the Community and improved information on the subject.

ARTICLE 2

1. The Commission, in close cooperation with the Member States, shall undertake work to fulfil the aims set out in Article 1 on the comparability of vocational training qualifications between the various Member States, in respect of specific occupations or groups of occupations.

2. The work may use as a reference the structure of training levels drawn up by the Commission with the help of the Advisory Committee for Vocational Training. The text of the said structure is attached to this Decision for information purposes.

3. The work referred to in paragraph 2 shall first and foremost concentrate on the occupational qualifications of skilled workers in mutually agreed occupations or groups of occupations.

4. The scope of this Decision may subsequently be extended to permit work to be undertaken, on a proposal from the Commission, at other levels of training.

5. The SEDOC register, used in connection with the European system for the international clearing of vacancies and applications for employment, shall, whenever possible, be used as the common frame of reference for vocational classifications.

ARTICLE 3

The following working procedure shall be employed by the Commission in establishing the comparability of vocational training qualifications in close cooperation with the Member States and the organisations of workers and employers at Community level:

1. selection of the relevant occupations or groups of occupations on a proposal from the Member States or the competent employer or worker organisations at Community level;
2. drawing up mutually agreed Community job descriptions for the occupations or groups of occupations referred to in the first indent;
3. matching the vocational training qualification recognised in the various Member States with the job descriptions referred to in the second indent;
4. establishing tables incorporating information on:
   (a) the SEDOC and national classification codes;
   (b) the level of vocational training;
   (c) for each Member State, the vocational title and corresponding vocational training qualifications;
   (d) the organisations and institutions responsible for dispensing vocational training;
   (e) the authorities and organisations competent to issue or to validate diplomas, certificates, or other documents certifying that vocational training has been acquired;
5. publication of the mutually agreed Community job descriptions and the comparative tables in the *Official Journal of the European Communities*;
6. establishment, within the meaning of Article 4(3), of a standard information sheet for each occupation or group of occupations, to be published in the *Official Journal of the European Communities*;
7. dissemination of information on the established comparabilities to all appropriate bodies at national, regional and local levels, as well as throughout the occupational sectors concerned.

This action could be supported by the creation of a Community-wide database, if experience shows the need for such a base.

ARTICLE 4

1. Each Member State shall designate a coordination body, based wherever possible on existing structures, which shall be responsible for ensuring – in close collaboration with the social partners and the occupational sectors concerned – the proper dissemination of information to all interested bodies. The Member States shall also designate the body responsible for contacts with the coordination bodies in other Member States and with the Commission.
2. The coordination bodies of the Member States shall be competent to establish appropriate arrangements with regard to vocational training information for their competent national, regional or local bodies, as well as for their own nationals wishing to work in other Member States and for workers who are nationals of other Member States, on established cases of comparable vocational qualifications.

3. The bodies referred to in paragraph 2 may supply on request in all Member States an information sheet drawn up in accordance with the model provided for in the sixth indent of Article 3, which the worker may present to the employer together with his national certificate.

4. The Commission is to continue studying the introduction of the European vocational training pass advocated by the Committee on a People's Europe in paragraph 21 of its report of 29 and 30 March 1985.

5. The Commission shall give the bodies referred to in paragraph 2, on request, all necessary assistance and advice concerning the preparation and setting-up of the arrangements provided for in paragraph 2, including the adaptation and checking of the relevant technical documents.

ARTICLE 5

The Commission shall, in close liaison with the national coordination bodies designated by the Member States,

1. review and update at appropriate, regular intervals, in close cooperation with the Member States and the organisations of workers and employers at Community level, the mutually agreed Community job descriptions and the comparative tables relating to the comparability of vocational training qualifications;

2. where necessary, formulate proposals for a more efficient operation of the system including other measures likely to improve the situation as regards the comparability of vocational qualification certificates;

3. where necessary, assist in the case of technical difficulties encountered by the national authorities of specialised bodies concerned.

ARTICLE 6

Each Member State shall submit to the Commission, for the first time two years after adoption of this Decision, and therefore every four years, a national report on the implementation of this Decision and the results obtained.

The Commission shall, at appropriate intervals, submit a report on its own work and on the application of this Decision in the Member States.

ARTICLE 7

This Decision is addressed to the Member States and the Commission.

Done at Brussels, 16 July 1985

For the Council
The President
M. Fischbach

(1) OJ 63, 20.4.1963, p. 1338/63.
(2) OJ C 77, 19.3.1984, p. 11.
(3) OJ C 35, 9.2.1984, p. 12.
(4) OJ C 98, 20.8.1974, p. 1.
(5) OJ C 193, 20.7.1983, p. 2.

ANNEX
Training-level structure referred to in Article 2(2)

LEVEL 1
Training providing access to this level: compulsory education and professional initiation.

This professional initiation is acquired at an educational establishment, in an out-of-school training programme, or at the undertaking. The volume of theoretical knowledge and practical capabilities involved is very limited.

This form of training must primarily enable the holder to perform relatively simple work and may be fairly quickly acquired.

LEVEL 2
Training providing access to this level: compulsory education and vocational training (including, in particular, apprenticeships). This level corresponds to a level where the holder is fully qualified to engage in a specific activity, with the capacity to use the instruments and techniques relating thereto.

This activity involves chiefly the performance of work which may be independent within the limits of the relevant techniques.

LEVEL 3
Training providing access to this level: compulsory education and/or vocational training and additional technical training or technical educational training, or other secondary level training.

This form of training involves a greater fund of theoretical knowledge than level 2. Activity involves chiefly technical work which can be performed independently and/or entail executive and coordination duties.

LEVEL 4
Training providing access to this level: secondary training (general or vocational) and post-secondary technical training.

This form of training involves high-level technical training acquired at or outside educational establishments. The resultant qualification covers a higher level of knowledge and of capabilities. It does not generally require mastery of the scientific bases of the various areas concerned. Such capabilities and knowledge make it possible in a generally autonomous or in an independent way to assume design and/or management and/or administrative responsibilities.

LEVEL 5
Training providing access to this level: secondary training (general or vocational) and complete higher training.

This form of training generally leads to an autonomously pursued vocational activity – as an employee or as a self-employed person – entailing a mastery of the scientific bases of the occupation. The qualifications required for engaging in a vocational activity may be integrated at these various levels.

Annex 3. The description format of national classification systems

A. Official data

1. Describe in short the 'history' of the (national) classification system(s) of vocational standards in operation in your country.
   - Which interests were taken into account?
   - Which aspects of earlier systems were or were not implemented in the system in operation?

2. Which definition of standards do you use?
   - What is regarded as a standard in your country, expressed in a possible format?
   - What are the elements of standards (state of the art, relevance for the future)?
   - Which types of standards are used (industry standards, enterprise standards, school-based standards) and are you using one or more standards?
   - How to avoid bias (i.e. avoidance of bias and discrimination of the elements, which procedures)?

3. About the definition of the classification system.
   - What is described in the classification system by definition and by component?
   - What elements are included in the system?
   - What is the number of levels which are used?
   - What is the definition of the levels used (i.e. the level descriptors)?
   - What are the criteria for the allocation of standards to levels?

4. About the scope and binding nature.
   - Does your country have a national classification system or a number of regional classification systems or even branch-specific systems?
   - If your country has specific regional or branch systems, where do they differ from each other?
   - What is the status of the system (mandatory or not)?

5. What are the official aims and function(s) of classification system(s) as well as the actual aims and function(s) or aims/functions to be obtained in the near future?

6. Which procedures for the development of standards were followed?
   - Which aspects of the procedure are regularised?
   - Which aspects are the subject of decision-making by the people involved?
   - Who has to be involved?

- Who should take the initiative to update standards?
- Do you use fixed and formal periods of validity of standards?
- Give a description of formal procedures or the most common procedures step by step.
- Which (standard) bodies are formally recognised for the purpose of developing and maintaining the standards?

7. Describe the procedures for the validation and implementation of standards.
   - Does your country have different procedures for the adaptation of standards and the implementation of new standards in the classification system?
   - Give a description of the procedure(s) step by step.

8. In which way are standards maintained?
   - Who is primarily responsible?
   - What is the period of reviewing the standards (maximum or minimum)?

9. Describe the similarities and differences between the system(s) used in your country and the European five-level structure.
   - Which number of levels?
   - Which definition of levels?
   - The criteria for allocation.

10. What is the way(s) in which the European five-level structure is (still) used in your country in addition to your 'national' system(s) for classification?

B. Case studies

1. Give a description of the procedure for the development of standards recently executed in two sectors (healthcare and the construction industry):
   - People involved (national, regional bodies, position, background, part in the process, responsibility).
   - Procedures step by step.
   - Time span.
   - Which aids and appliances, resources and instruments were used.
2. Describe the procedure(s) for the validation of standards in these two sectors.
3. Describe the assessment of the procedures by people directly involved.
   - Workability of the steps and criteria for classification.
   - Compromises negotiated.
   - Opinion of the quality of the results.
   - Bottlenecks and other emerging problems caused by the implementation.

C. Give your personal (expert) opinion about:

1. Positive and negative aspects of the classification system in your country procedures and classification criteria included.
2. The potentials of the classification system to be used for accreditation of prior learning.
   - What should be changed to enhance these potentials?

Description of ISCED-97 levels, classification criteria and subcategories

LEVELS OF EDUCATION AT A GLANCE

HOW TO DETERMINE THE LEVEL OF A PROGRAMME

PROXY CRITERIA FOR CONTENT		NAME OF THE LEVEL	CODE	COMPLEMENTARY
MAIN CRITERIA	SUBSIDIARY CRITERIA			DIMENSIONS
Educational properties School or centre-based Minimum age Upper age limit	Staff qualification	Pre-primary education	0	None
Beginning of systematic apprenticeship of reading, writing and mathematics	Entry into the nationally designated primary institutions or programmes Start of compulsory education	Primary education First stage of basic education	1	None
Subject presentation Full implementation of basic skills and foundation for lifelong learning	Entry after some six years of primary education End of the cycle after nine years since the beginning of primary education End of compulsory education Several teachers conduct classes in their field of specialisation	Lower secondary education Second stage of basic education	2	Type of subsequent education or destination Programme orientation
Typical entrance qualification Minimum entrance requirement		(Upper) secondary education	3	Type of subsequent education or destination. Programme orientation. Cumulative duration since the beginning of ISCED level 3.

H O W   T O   D E T E R M I N E   T H E   L E V E L   O F   A   P R O G R A M M E

| PROXY CRITERIA FOR CONTENTS | | NAME OF THE LEVEL | CODE | COMPLEMENTARY |
MAIN CRITERIA	SUBSIDIARY CRITERIA			DIMENSIONS
Entrance requirement, Content Age Duration		Post-secondary non-tertiary education	4	Type of subsequent education or destination Cumulative duration since the beginning of ISCED level 3 Programme orientation
Minimum entrance requirement, Type of certification obtained Duration		First stage of tertiary education (not leading directly to an advanced research qualification)	5	Type of programmes Cumulative theoretical duration at tertiary-level National degree and qualification structure.
Research-oriented content Submission of thesis or dissertation	Prepare graduates for faculty and research posts	Second stage of tertiary education (leading to an advanced research qualification)	6	None

ISCED CLASSIFICATION (old)

The international standard classification of education (ISCED) was designed by Unesco in the early 1970s and adopted in 1978. It was 'to serve as an instrument suitable for assembling, compiling and presenting statistics of education both within individual countries and internationally'. In December 1997, Unesco agreed on a new ISCED. The description of the 'old' ISCED levels (Eurostat statistics) are as follows.

ISCED level 0 (pre-primary education)

Education preceding primary education. In the vast majority of cases, it is not compulsory.

ISCED level 1 (primary education)

Begins between the ages of four and seven, is compulsory in all cases and lasts five or six years as a rule.

ISCED level 2 (lower secondary education)

Compulsory schooling in all European countries. The end of this level often corresponds to the end of full-time compulsory school.

ISCED level 3 (upper secondary education)

Begins around the age of 14 or 15 and refers to either general, technical or vocational education. It may lead to the standard required for admission to higher education or it may be 'terminal', as is sometimes the case with vocational education and training.

ISCED levels 5, 6, 7 (higher education)

ISCED level 5 covers programmes which generally do not lead to the awarding of a university degree or equivalent, but admission to this level usually requires the successful completion of a programme at the upper secondary level.

ISCED level 6 covers programmes leading to a first university degree or equivalent.

ISCED level 7 covers programmes leading to a second, postgraduate university degree.

Annex 5. List of abbreviations and acronyms

ACAC	The *Awdurdof Cwricwlwm ac Asesu Cymru*, Wales (Curriculum and Assessment Authority for Wales)
ACOA	*Advies Commissie Onderwijs Arbeidsmarkt* (Independent Vocational Education and Labour Market Advisory Committee, the Netherlands)
AES	*Accuerdo Económico y Social* (economic and social agreement, Spain)
APL	Accreditation of prior learning
BEP	*Brevets d'études professionnelles* (vocational studies certificate, France)
BIBB	*Bundesinstitut für Berufsbildung* (Federal Institute for Vocational Training, Germany)
CAP	*Certificat d'aptitude professionnelle* (certificate of vocational aptitude, France)
Catalogue of FPR qualifications	Syllabus of regulated vocational training (Spain)
CCEA	Council for the Curriculum, Examinations and Assessment
Cedefop	European Centre for the Development of Vocational Training
CEP	*Certificat d'éducation professionnelle* (certificate of vocational education, France)
CEREQ	*Centre d'études et de recherches sur les qualifications* (Centre for Study and Research on Qualifications, France)
CGFP	*Consejo General de la Formación Profesional* (General Council for Vocational Training, Spain)
CINOP	*Centrum voor de Innovatie van Opleidingen* (Centre for the Innovation of Education and Training, the Netherlands)
CIREM	*Centre d'iniciatives I Recerques Europees a la Mediterania* (Foundation Centre for European Initiatives and Research in the Mediterranean, Spain)
Ciretoq	Cedefop's network for research cooperation on trends in occupations and qualifications
CPC	*Commissions professionnelles consultatives* (occupational professional advisory committees, France)

CQP	*Certificats de qualifications professionnelles* (vocational qualification certificates, France)
CTH	*Commission technique d'homologation des titres et diplômes* (Technical Commission for the Accreditation of Diplomas and Certificates, France)
CTP	*Catálogo de Títulos Profesionales* (catalogue of all the titles of regulated vocational training, Spain)
DESCO	*Direction de l'enseignement scolaire* (Directorate for School Education, France)
DfEE	Department for Education and Employment (UK)
DUT	*Diplômes Universitaires Technologiques* (technical university diplomas, France)
EU	European Union
EURES	European employment services
FPR	*Formación profesional reglada* (regulated vocational training, Spain)
GCSE	General certificate of secondary education
GNVQ	General national vocational qualification
INEM	*Instituto Nacional de Empleo* (National Office for Employment, Spain)
ISCED	International standard classification of education
IUT	*Instituts universitaires de technologie* (university institutes for technology, France)
KMK	*Ständige Konferenz der Kultusminister der Länder* (Standing Conference of Education Ministers of the Federal States, Germany)
LOB	*Landelijk Orgaan Beroepsonderwijs* (National Body for Vocational Education, the Netherlands)
LOGSE	*Ley de Ordenación General del Sistema Educativo* (law on the general regulation of the education system, Spain)
MBO	*Middelbaar beroepsonderwijs* (senior secondary vocational education, the Netherlands)
MEC	Ministry of Education and Culture (Spain)
NTO	National training organisation

NVQ	National vocational qualification
OECD	Organisation for Economic Cooperation and Development
PCS	*Professions et catégories socio-professionnelles* (occupations and socio-professional categories, France)
QCA	Qualifications and Curriculum Authority
RVQ	Review of vocational qualifications (England)
SEDOC	*Système Européen de diffusion des offres et des demandes d'emploi en compensation internationale* (European system for the distribution of international job offers and demands)
SNC	*Sistema nacional de cualificaciones* (national system of qualifications, Spain)
SVQ	Scottish vocational qualification
Unesco	United Nations Educational, Scientific, and Cultural Organisation
VET	Vocational education and training

Cedefop (European Centre for the Development of Vocational Training)

European structures
of qualification levels

**A synthesis based on reports on recent developments
in Germany, Spain, France, the Netherlands
and the United Kingdom (England and Wales)
VOLUME 1**

Anneke Westerhuis

Luxembourg:
Office for Official Publications of the European Communities

2001 – VI, 116 pp. – 17.5 x 25 cm

(Cedefop Reference series; 20 – ISSN 1608-7089)

Price (excluding VAT) in Luxembourg: EUR 8.50

No of publication: 3016 EN